Creative
COASTAL
Cooking

*Recipes from a dozen contemporary restaurants
along the coast of Maine*

by Terry Ward Libby

ISBN 0892726105

Designed by Chilton Creative
Cover photographs: Walter Bibikow/GettyImages, Steve Cohen/Getty Images
Interior photographs: Terry Ward Libby

1   2   3   4   5

Printed by Versa Press Inc.
East Peoria, Illinois

Down East Books
P.O. Box 679
Camden, ME 04843
BOOK ORDERS: 1-800-685-7962

Library of Congress Card Number: 2003106539

Contents

Acknowledgments

If a dozen chefs in Maine hadn't trusted me with all those recipes—their stock in trade—you wouldn't be reading this, or eating so well.

My thanks to Kerry Altiero, Ev Donnelly, Nora Cavin, Herbert and Eleanor Peters, Julie Harris, Julie Berberian, Susanne Hathaway, Lise Desrochers, Patti Savoie, Allison Martin, Elmer Beal, Frances Holdgate, Jay Villani, David Noyes, Abby Harmon, Lynne Leavitt, Ralph McDonnell, Anna Durand, Cherie Davis, Melissa Kelly, and Wendy Hebb. Thanks also to Chris Cornell and Amy Sutherland for their good advice in the early planning stages of this project.

My husband, Tony Libby, traveled with me along the coast as I prepared to put this book together. He took all the pictures. He has a good eye for people and places, and never once complained about having to visit all those beautiful towns and eat all those great meals.

Introduction

During the autumns of 2001 and 2002, I traveled north along the Atlantic coast from southern Maine to Bar Harbor looking for owner-operated cafés and restaurants with inventive menus. I was looking for cooking styles rooted in New England tradition, but was willing to venture into some new territory as long as the result was simple and delicious: modern comfort food, if you will. I looked for chef-owners who use local produce and fish from local waters, who value their ties to the surrounding community, and who view their restaurants as more than just business enterprises.

What I found was a generation of young entrepreneurs who are feeding both the locals and the tourists, in the process defining a new coastal cuisine for Maine by bringing inventive stuff like organic foods and ethnic seasonings and cooking methods to the traditional repertoire.

Many of the people I met are artists as well as chefs, transplants from big urban areas with great stories to tell. Others are from Maine families with deep roots—farmers and fishermen. Their restaurants are mostly sweat-equity enterprises; some are in buildings rescued from ruin, some in town, some off the beaten path. They do it to share a passion for food and as an expression of who they are.

Twelve generous chefs agreed to take on this project with me. This cookbook will introduce them to you, along with their restaurants, their families, and communities, by way of some snapshots, a little history, and a little geography. It's good to put a face to the recipe—food is always better when it's shared with friends.

—TERRY WARD LIBBY

About the recipes

As a rule, directions for preparing each recipe in Creative Coastal Cooking are given in numbered steps, though some of the recipes are so simple that instructions are provided in a few sentences. Any recipe not attributed to a specific chef or restaurant is one from my own collection of favorites, provided as a "variation" on recipes provided by my collaborators.

Twelve Restaurants in Maine

FROM KENNEBUNK TO BAR HARBOR

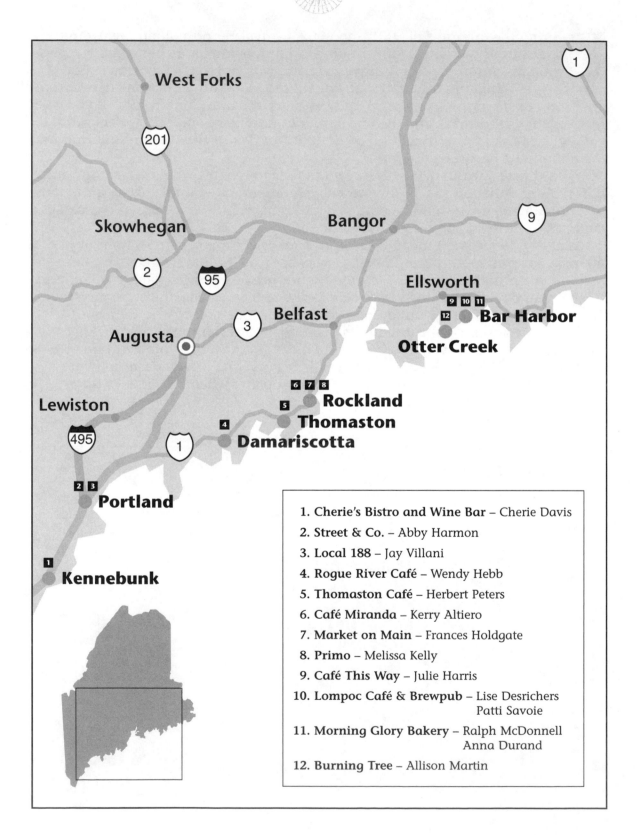

1. **Cherie's Bistro and Wine Bar** – Cherie Davis
2. **Street & Co.** – Abby Harmon
3. **Local 188** – Jay Villani
4. **Rogue River Café** – Wendy Hebb
5. **Thomaston Café** – Herbert Peters
6. **Café Miranda** – Kerry Altiero
7. **Market on Main** – Frances Holdgate
8. **Primo** – Melissa Kelly
9. **Café This Way** – Julie Harris
10. **Lompoc Café & Brewpub** – Lise Desrichers
    Patti Savoie
11. **Morning Glory Bakery** – Ralph McDonnell
    Anna Durand
12. **Burning Tree** – Allison Martin

Cherie's Bistro and Wine Bar

7 HIGH STREET, KENNEBUNK

Most tourists pass through Kennebunk on their way to crowded Kennebunkport, bypassing the charms of this historic town with a year-round population of twelve thousand. It was first settled in 1603. Today Kennebunk's citizens are determined to preserve the character and natural beauty of the place—20 percent of the town has been designated conservation land and open space. Summer Street is lined with restored mansions, the homes of sea captains from another era. "It's a classic New England village," says Kennebunk town manager Barry Tibbetts. "I wouldn't want to live anyplace else.

"In Maine, we like to say that we live 'life the way it should be,' and that's not just a cliché," Tibbetts continues. "Every town has a place best known to the locals, a stellar bakery or restaurant. If you ask anyone on the street in Kennebunk where to eat, they're going to send you to Cherie's."

Cherie Davis has built a reputation on her deli-bakery, Sweet Treats, and the adjacent Cherie's Bistro and Wine Bar where she uses local, seasonal products to create inventive and elegant entrées.

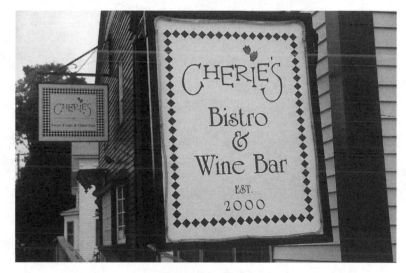

Cherie's in Kennebunk

Street & Co.

33 WHARF STREET, PORTLAND

Few towns in America have such salty air as Portland. The restored Old Port district revels in its maritime past, and down one of its cobblestoned alleyways you'll find Street & Co., a warehouse converted by owner Dana Street into a restaurant rich with rustic atmosphere. In the kitchen is chef Abby Harmon, a no-nonsense professional who creates an original seafood-only menu every night. Abby works directly with Street & Co.'s seafood "forager"—a person whose sole job it is to seek out the best raw seafood to be had in Portland on any given day.

"It is so important for me always to give credit to my whole kitchen crew, especially to Riley Shyrock, my sous-chef. Without them I wouldn't be able to create half the food I do at Street & Co."

—CHEF ABBY HARMON

Street & Co. in Portland's Old Port

Local 188

Just as its name implies, Local 188 is home to an informal union of artists and an eatery that feels rooted in the neighborhood it calls home, Portland's Arts District.

Few restaurants enjoy the kind of positive street buzz that Local 188 has generated since it opened in Portland in the spring of 1999. It grew from an art gallery and sometime tapas bar into a full-time, Spanish-inspired restaurant. Local 188 is still part gallery. Here you'll dine surrounded by sculpture and paintings by Portland artists. It draws a dinner crowd every night and is one of Portland's favorite Sunday brunch destinations.

Owner and head cook Jay Villani lets instinct take over in the kitchen. His favorite ingredients are the staples of Basque and Spanish cuisine—Romesco sauce, saffron, shellfish—dishes easily reproduced with Maine's native harvest of seafood and produce.

Local 188 in Portland's Arts District

Rogue River Café

155 MAIN STREET, DAMARISCOTTA

Heading north along Route 1 from Portland to the Midcoast, you will come to Damariscotta, an idyllic coastal town on the Damariscotta River, just about five miles from the open ocean. Do not resist the urge for a detour through town and a stop at Rogue River Café.

"This was once a thriving shipbuilding town, famous for its swift clipper ships. Damariscotta—pronounced dama-ris-COT-ta—is the Abenaki word for 'plenty of alewives,' meaning plenty of little herrings. This is where you can see the famous Damariscotta Oyster Shell Heaps, accumulated over two thousand years as the Penobscot Indians gathered for celebrations and to feast on the local shellfish.

"Rogue River Café is a great place to meet friends old and new. There's a feeling of warmth from the moment you walk in the door. The community suppers that were started there last year are wonderful events that rally the town for causes that we feel strongly about, while giving us a nice chance to visit, too."

—HEATHER O'BRYAN, DIRECTOR, DAMARISCOTTA REGION CHAMBER OF COMMERCE

Rogue River Cafe on picturesque Main Street, Damariscotta

Our Town Dinners at Rogue River Café

"Rogue River opened as Rogue River Food and Supply in July 2000 in a space that had for thirty-five years housed Belknap's Hardware Store. The building has been in the same family for more than sixty-five years. We restored it to its original integrity, stripping out wallboard that covered beautiful old locally made brick, exposing the original overhead beams, and pulling away worn linoleum to find pine-plank floors. The upstairs, which earlier housed a forge where nails and other hardware were made, became a public space, and the old hearth was rebuilt.

"Initially, my concept was to sell antiques related to cooking in the upper level of the store, and prepared foods for take out in the lower level, like picnics packed in Vermont-made baskets. There were a few tables provided for patrons who wanted to eat their pastries or lunch on the premises, but soon I realized that guests were finding space throughout the store, pushing aside merchandise and pulling up wobbly old chairs, just to sit down and eat at Rogue River. We quickly became Rogue River Café. Now we serve lunch and dinner upstairs and cater events on premises and off.

"Our Town Dinners offer a homemade meal, served family style, with tables pulled together and set with heaping platters of food fresh from the kitchen. Locals and visitors pay twelve dollars a plate to join in, and the proceeds go to a designated community-based nonprofit. The community turns out and has a great gathering, dispelling the sense of isolation that the long, dark Maine winters can sometimes bring on."

—WENDY HEBB, ROGUE RIVER CAFÉ OWNER AND COMMUNITY SERVICE AWARD RECIPIENT

Thomaston Café

154 MAIN STREET, THOMASTON

"In the fall of 1989, a student in my culinary program at the Midcoast School of Technology in Rockland asked me to help him open a coffee shop in his hometown of Thomaston. I had no good reason not to help him.

"So I began to help with renovations to the old storefront on Route 1, Main Street, in Thomaston. The only problem was that his money wasn't available until later, or so I was told. Soon he disappeared. My wife, Eleanor, and I had already invested five thousand dollars in the place, so we decided to start the Thomaston Café and Bakery.

"It took months to complete the renovations—but we opened at last in April 1990. Right from the beginning we decided to prepare all our foods ourselves from the best available ingredients and, if possible, from local growers and producers. The first two years, I would start work every morning at 4 A.M. and leave three hours later for my teaching job in Rockland. Eleanor managed the restaurant while I was away—she did the cooking, baking, waiting on tables, and the thousand other things that come up in a day at a busy restaurant.

"It didn't take long for the word to spread. Soon we could count on regular customers from as far north as Camden, the peninsulas of St. George, Cushing, Friendship, and as far south as Damariscotta. Sundays, especially, became a great hit with eggs Benedict, omelets, Belgian waffles, and champagne mimosas made with fresh orange juice.

"In 1998 I decided to retire from teaching and put all my efforts into the café. We added candlelit dinners on Friday and Saturday nights with special dishes like island crab cakes, roasted pheasant, grilled lamb chops.

"I do the cooking myself, now with the help of my son, Peter."

—HERBERT PETERS, CHEF-OWNER, THOMASTON CAFÉ

*Herbert and Eleanor Peters
at Thomaston Café*

Peter Peters

Café Miranda

15 OAK STREET, ROCKLAND

No chef in Maine brings more spirit, passion, or theatricality into the kitchen than Kerry Altiero, chef-owner of Café Miranda. His motto: "We do not serve the food of cowards." Every night he offers up a long menu of wholly original dishes, all roasted in his custom-designed wood-fired brick oven. The best seats in the house are the four at the bar that overlook the oven and the preparation of every plate by Altiero.

He disdains the current popularity of "fusion" cuisine, but admits to taking a lot of creative license in the kitchen himself:

"Before your Mexican grandma comes over to beat me with a stick, I have to say that we 'interpret' food. I often say that we are unencumbered by classicism, exact knowledge, and travel experience. But we do have soul…plus ten years of experience and a lot of onions. To leverage flavor, an onion is your best friend.

"From the start, we've been blessed with a long-term professional crew that pulls it off five days a week, no matter what. We make kick-ass food in a ton of styles while respecting the ethnic basis—most of the time—of every dish we invent. We're creative, yes, but we try not to muddle or overstylize what we do. We want our customers to eat like hungry workers in a comfy café setting. That's the objective.

"This, of course, leads to a massive menu that we change pretty much daily. We introduce new stuff all the time, along with 'archival dishes' the regulars won't let us forget. Our style is limited only by our equipment, the raw ingredients we can scavenge every day, and our imaginations. We love to stir that pot."

—KERRY ALTIERO, CHEF-OWNER, CAFÉ MIRANDA

Café Miranda, Rockland

Chef Kerry Altiero

<u>Nora Cavin's Notes on Café Miranda</u>

". . . I sit at the 'bar' and watch the head chef flinging stuff into the brick oven, heaving in the occasional log, pulling stuff out again, a kind of hectic choreography as he and the sous-chef behind him feint around each other in what space there is, assemble the dishes, grab tongfuls of fixings from the rows of little cooled and heated metal wells in the counter opposite the oven, squirt stuff from squeeze bottles, sprinkle on this and that. Quite a show. And very good food, and lots of it.

". . . I'm in Rockland in October, spend a good several evenings chez Café Miranda, and Kerry tells me about this upcoming improvisational wine-tasting dinner. Small crowd, dining together family-style-esque, on a Sunday, when Miranda would ordinarily be closed. Tony Coturri, California winemaker whose wines they serve, will crack open a bottle, everyone gets a taste, suggestions will be entertained, based on which Kerry and Chris, the sous-chef, will create dishes in harmony with/in contrast to/inspired by that tasted bottle, from their considerable array of provisions. And on to the next. 'We will continue till reason forces us to stop,' says the promotional card. Nothing quite like this has ever been tried, so far as any of the parties know. 'You've got to be there,' Kerry tells me."

Writer Nora Cavin, a Miranda regular

Market on Main, MOM

315 Main Street, Rockland

Market on Main, also known to Rockland locals as MOM, opened in downtown Rockland in the summer of 1999. It's a hub of social activity and a community gathering place that feeds the locals three squares a day—breakfast, lunch, and dinner. Its wide deli case offers up big platters and bowls of scratch-made food from the kitchen run by Frances Holdgate and her staff. MOM's mission: to serve and provide handcrafted quality food at an affordable price. Mission accomplished.

In MOM's kitchen   *Rockland Harbor*

Primo

2 SOUTH MAIN STREET, ROUTE 73, ROCKLAND

Primo embodies the spirit of the young entrepreneurs who created it—chef Melissa Kelly and baker Price Kushner. The restaurant is housed in a simple farmhouse on the outskirts of Rockland, the interior sumptuously restored, with bedrooms and parlors converted to intimate dining rooms upstairs and down. Surrounding the house is a network of organic gardens where Melissa picks the vegetables in the morning that will find their way to diners' plates that night.

Melissa is a chef with many accolades. She graduated first in her class at the Culinary Institute of America, has appeared on national television, and has won a James Beard Foundation award as most outstanding chef in the northeastern United States. She worked alongside the famous Alice Waters, owner of California's Chez Panisse Restaurant, who embraced the concept of "foraging" for pure regional ingredients and spurred a national movement among restaurateurs to consider the origin and integrity of the raw foods and products they use. It's a philosophy that Maine's chefs have embraced wholeheartedly, none more so than Melissa Kelly and Price Kushner.

Creative Coastal Cooking

Rockin' Rockland—The Midcoast

The Midcoast region dares to bill itself "the real Maine." Its complex coastline of dramatic peninsulas, broad bays, and unspoiled offshore islands has always been less crowded, less developed, than points to the north and south.

"Fifteen years ago all you came to Rockland for was a beer and a beatin', but today we have the Farnsworth and a downtown area that is absolutely arts-driven," says Bob Hastings, chamber of commerce director.

Though it is still a working fishing port with a beautiful harbor for its center-piece, Rockland has evolved into an arts mecca and business-friendly town as well. The Farnsworth Art Museum, in the heart of town, is the permanent home to the Maine in America exhibition and features the work of artists N. C. Wyeth and Jamie Wyeth—still a local resident who lives on an island off the St. George Peninsula. Rockland's refurbished Main Street is flanked at one end by the new corporate campus of MBNA, and at the other by the tony Samoset Resort.

Despite all its growth and newly acquired sophistication, Rockland remains a wonderfully livable town.

"It's a healthy mix of real people and real places, and food is definitely happening here," says Hastings. "I love Café Miranda, and what they're doing at Primo is amazing. We've had features in the *New York Times*, on the 'Food Network.' I honestly believe you can find the best food in the country right here."

The front porch at Primo

Café This Way

14 ½ MOUNT DESERT STREET, BAR HARBOR

Café This Way was created in 1997 by three humble young women who are quick to give credit for their success to each other, and to their big community of friends and coworkers. Julie Harris, Julie Berberian, and Susanne Hathaway gutted the inside of the wood-frame building that is home to the café and did the renovation work themselves, creating a big cozy dining room that's more like a den, with bookcases and a big stone hearth.

Café This Way is, above all, playful. It's a bit hard to find, set back from the main drag in perpetually crowded downtown Bar Harbor, thus the name and the logo—a friendly hand that points the way. The tables all have comic themes developed by employees past and present—Wonder Woman, Charlie's Angels, the 1970s, Elvis—with pictures laminated right into the tabletops for the amusement of diners. The café has a whole collection of original cartoons expertly drawn by the staff, depicting the perils of waiting tables for a living. See the Web site www.cafethisway.com for a sampling of these.

But when it comes to food, head chef Julie Harris can get pretty serious. Her fish entrées are standouts because she respects the natural flavors of the local catch and seasons her seafood with a light hand.

Café This Way operates by a rule that many restaurants might do well to mimic. They serve breakfast and dinner—no lunches. A line forms at the door every morning for hot coffee, fresh baked goods, and Julie's incredible scratch-made corned beef hash. Who needs lunch?

Julie Berberian, Susanne Hathaway, Chef Julie Harris
Owners, Café This Way

Lompoc Café & Brewpub

36 RODICK STREET, BAR HARBOR

I n the kitchen at Lompoc Café, Lise Desrochers and Patti Savoie specialize in home-style comfort foods—great soups, stews, and other hearty fare, spiced with southwestern and Mediterranean flavors that pair nicely with Lompoc's long menu of microbrews.

"In 1991 Lompoc Café was the original home of Bar Harbor's first local beer maker, the Acadia Brewing Company. That's when our signature brew, Bar Harbor Real Ale, was first produced. In the years since, Acadia Brewing Company became Atlantic Brewing Company. They now produce at least five regular types of beer, plus the occasional seasonal brew. The Atlantic Brewing Company is now located in Town Hill, about seven miles from downtown Bar Harbor. We are still affiliated, though no longer under one ownership. At the Lompoc, we carry the Atlantic Brewing Company's great microbrews—the Real Ale, Bar Harbor Blueberry Ale, Coal Porter, Island Ginger, Special Old Bitter or 'S.O.B.,' and Brother Adams Bragget, a honey-flavored ale."

—PATTI SAVOIE, OWNER, LOMPOC CAFÉ

The Bocce Court at Lompoc Café

Morning Glory Bakery

39 RODICK STREET, BAR HARBOR

The crew at neighboring Café This Way in Bar Harbor are great fans of talented bakers Ralph McDonnell and Anna Durand, owners of Morning Glory Bakery. A smart restaurateur knows that if you don't have a good hand at baking yourself, you should find someone who does. Morning Glory produces breads for many of Bar Harbor's restaurants, including Café This Way.

Everything is made 100 percent from scratch, a fact that's easily witnessed by anyone who drops by, since Morning Glory's big baking kitchen is completely open to public view. The breads and pastries here are of the hearty sort—chunky muffins and cookies, pies and cakes. The counter opens at 7 A.M. for baked goods, hot coffee, and smoothies, with sandwiches and boxed lunches made to order in the afternoons.

Creative Coastal Cooking

Burning Tree

71 OTTER CREEK DRIVE, ROUTE 3, OTTER CREEK

Elmer Beal on serving seafood from local waters at the Burning Tree:

"Whenever we travel, we love to visit seaside towns and look for local seafood—whatever is being landed nearby and is sparkling fresh. Unfortunately, like so much of the food in our country—which travels an average of three thousand miles before it reaches the consumer—many of those restaurants are serving seafood that came from across the country or across the globe. We began the Burning Tree largely because we wanted to be one of those places that kindred souls would find and be delighted by.

"Really fresh, wild fish is amazingly healthy food and almost melts in the mouth with its juices, textures, and flavors. Frozen, it is simply not the same, especially the groundfish—flaky fishes like cod, flounder, sole, and haddock. The moisture just abandons them when they are frozen and thawed. There are places far from the sea where we would probably prefer the frozen fish, but not at the coast.

"As the world's population has demanded more and more of this great food, many groundfish stocks have declined, and seaside people's quality of life has declined along with them. Rebuilding these stocks has imposed many sacrifices on those who love fish, especially those who catch it. A great number of Maine's groundfishermen are now sitting on the sidelines, some are out of business, and those who remain fish fewer than eighty days per year.

"Fortunately for us and our customers, most of the remaining small boats fish their few days during the summer season when Burning Tree is open for business. By keeping track of their schedules by cell phone, we can know when their fish are going to auction and can supply ourselves with the freshest. Since our fishermen are responsibly observing all of the federally mandated conservation measures, we feel they deserve all of the support they can get. We sell their fish with enthusiasm and pride. Buying whole fish helps us to better judge quality, but at the same time means that we have to fillet them ourselves—one more thing we do to assure our customers of the best.

In the kitchen at the Burning Tree, Aaron Steiner and Jacob Oakes

"On a typical night, we will offer seven or eight different species of fish and six other types of seafood, including quahogs, hen clams, scallops, mussels, crab, and lobster, all in different preparations and some in more than one preparation. In order to keep this perishable inventory moving, we offer only five entrées that are not seafood, three of which are vegetarian. We are very careful not to overstock. We think every item on our menu is special and exciting, so we don't panic if we run out of something. If we do, that just means we were careful to keep it fresh.

"Our commitment to serving the best available foods allows us to support our local economy. We extend this to the vegetables and poultry we serve as well. Wherever we can, we use local and organic produce. We have several gardens scattered throughout our neighborhood that supply our herbs, lettuce, greens, and other items, which we love to grow."

Elmer is a professor of anthropology at the College of the Atlantic in Bar Harbor, where he studies and writes on the subjects of organic and sustainable agriculture, and Maine's fishing and timber industries. He and his wife, chef Allison Martin, are the owner-operators of the Burning Tree Restaurant.

In the garden at the Burning Tree,
Casey Hannifin, Addie Beal,
and Riley McIsaac

Creative Coastal Cooking

The Recipes

Chapter 1

Starters and Appetizers

DIPS AND SPREADS, NEW FONDUES,
MEAT AND SEAFOOD SMALL PLATES

Rockland Harbor

Monterey Jack and Chipotle Cheese Sauce

Lompoc Café, Bar Harbor

makes about 4 cups

This versatile and delicious sauce started as a sandwich spread for a Lompoc Café lunch special, and graduated to become the base sauce for spicy "white" pizzas. Serve it drizzled over char-grilled or baked chicken or shrimp (see Index), fried fish fillets, or hot tortilla chips. At room temperature it becomes a smooth, creamy dip. The chipotle chiles have plenty of heat, so if you prefer a mild sauce, go easy on them.

> 8 ounces cream cheese, softened
> 2 cups heavy cream
> 1 ½ teaspoons ground cumin
> ½ teaspoon salt
> ¼ cup puréed chipotle chiles in adobo sauce (or 2 tablespoons for mild sauce)
> 1 tablespoon minced fresh garlic
> 2 tablespoons Wondra flour
> 2 cups grated Monterey Jack cheese ("Pepper Jack" is optional)
> ¼ cup finely chopped fresh cilantro

1. In a sturdy saucepan, whisk the first 6 ingredients together over medium-high heat until melted and smooth.
2. Sprinkle in the Wondra while whisking, then add the grated cheese, stirring until thickened and hot. Remove from the heat and stir in the cilantro.

Note: Canned chipotle chile peppers packed in smoky adobo sauce are a staple of the Mexican kitchen. Look for them in specialty food markets and some supermarkets.

Shrimp Broiled in Monterey Jack and Chipotle Cheese Sauce
(cover recipe)

serves 4 as an appetizer (2 as a main course)

> 2 tablespoons unsalted butter, at room temperature
> 12 large raw shrimp, shelled and deveined
> 1 cup prepared Monterey Jack and Chipotle Cheese Sauce at room temperature (above)
> 3 tablespoons fine fresh breadcrumbs
> 2 cups cooked, warm orzo pasta
> 1 tablespoon chopped fresh parsley
> lemon wedges to garnish

1. Preheat the broiler set for high heat for 10 minutes. Use all the butter to grease a flameproof baking dish just large enough to hold all the shrimp in a single layer.
2. In a mixing bowl, toss the shrimp with the sauce, then spread the mixture in the baking dish. Dust evenly with the bread crumbs.
3. Broil for about 6 to 8 minutes, or until the bread crumbs are golden and the sauce is bubbly.
4. Divide the pasta among four small plates, top each with three shrimp, and drizzle on additional sauce from the baking dish. Garnish with the parsley and lemon wedges and serve immediately.

Roasted Cheese Plates— "New Fondues"

CAFÉ MIRANDA, ROCKLAND

each recipe serves 4 as an appetizer

Plates of oven-roasted cheese garnished with vegetables and herbs are a favorite appetizer at Café Miranda. It's like "fondue for the new millennium," says Kerry Altiero, "only better." Couldn't be simpler. No fussy fondue pots required— serve this right out of the oven with crusty bread.

Kerry recommends serving with a glass of wine or a pint of Geary's Pale Ale from Portland, and Henry Mancini's greatest hits.

Note: You must have a sturdy, ovenproof baking dish or platter for these recipes, because they're roasted at maximum temperature. Place an oven rack in the lower third of the oven, then preheat the oven to 450°F for 10 minutes. When ready to roast the cheese, turn the broiler on high, then quickly place the prepared dish in the oven. Watch it carefully, because oven temperatures vary and the "fondue" can go from bubbly to burned in no time.

Baked Cheddar and Roasted Garlic Fondue

8 cloves roasted garlic (see Index), peeled and chopped
8 ounces thickly sliced sharp Cheddar cheese
6 or 8 "grape" tomatoes tossed in 1 teaspoon olive oil
2 large basil leaves, slivered
a pinch of kosher salt
fresh-cracked black pepper

Distribute the garlic inside the dish, then arrange the cheese on top in a layer of overlapping slices. Top with the tomatoes and basil. Set the plate aside to allow the cheese to reach room temperature before roasting (about 30 minutes). Once in the oven, the fondue will be ready in 3 to 5 minutes. Season with the salt and pepper. Kerry recommends serving a Geary's Pale Ale from Portland with this one.

Stop and Smell the Gorgonzola

Only real Italian Gorgonzola has the creamy texture you'll want in this dish.

4 ounces imported Gorgonzola dolce, at room temperature
1 roasted red pepper, peeled and cut into strips (see Index)
2 large basil leaves, slivered

Spread the Gorgonzola over the dish, top with pepper strips and basil, and roast as directed above. Serve with a bottle of Sangiovese or other Tuscan red.

Queso Chorizo

1 large poblano pepper, seeded and cut into strips
¼ cup corn kernels, fresh-cut or thawed
¼ cup very thinly sliced red onion
1 tablespoon olive oil
4 ounces good Monterey Jack cheese, cut into ½-inch-thick slices
4 ounces cooked chorizo sausage, crumbled
1 lime, cut into thick wedges

1. Toss the pepper strips, corn, and onion with the olive oil and spread in the baking dish.
2. Place the cheese slices in a single layer over the vegetables, then sprinkle on the chorizo. Roast as directed above and serve with lime wedges and warm tortillas.

Baked Brie with Asparagus and Nuts

8 ounces ripe Brie or Camembert, cut into ½-inch-thick slices
8 spears fresh asparagus, brushed with olive oil
a pinch of kosher salt
¼ cup slivered almonds, or walnut or pecan halves, lightly toasted (see below)
lemon wedges

Arrange the cheese slices in the baking dish and set aside at room temperature for about 1 hour. Arrange the asparagus spears on top, season with salt, and roast as directed above until the cheese is completely melted and the asparagus has browned just a bit. Remove from the oven and top with nuts. Serve with lemon wedges and European-style bread.

Toasting Nuts

This can be done in a hot, dry skillet, on a baking tray in a toaster oven, or in a regular oven at 350°F. Nuts toast very quickly—in just 4 to 7 minutes—and must be watched so that they do not burn. They are done when they take on just a little toasty color and become fragrant. Remove them from the hot pan as soon as they are done, cool them on a plate, then store in an airtight container.

Baked Asiago Plate

CAFÉ THIS WAY, BAR HARBOR

serves 2–4

"This appetizer is called 'The Littlebit' on our menu. It was named after our friend Elizabeth, whose name had somehow been reduced to Littlebit, and as you can see, it's an appetizer with a little bit of this, and a little bit of that."

—CHEF JULIE HARRIS

Italian Asiago is a favorite cheese at Café This Way, but French raclette would be another good choice in this recipe because it melts to a smooth, spreadable consistency. This recipe can easily be doubled for a larger gathering. A good glass of wine is a must.

12 cloves garlic
1 tablespoon olive oil
8 ounces Asiago cheese, thinly sliced
½ cup roasted red peppers (see Index), drained and cut into strips
½ cup pitted kalamata olives

1. Preheat the oven to 350°F.
2. To roast the garlic cloves, place them in a small ovenproof dish and drizzle with the olive oil. Cover the dish tightly with foil and bake for 20 minutes, until the cloves are soft and brown.
3. In the center of an ovenproof plate, fan out the cheese slices in a single layer. Arrange the red pepper strips, olives, and roasted garlic cloves in three separate piles around the edge of the plate. Bake for about 10 minutes, or until the cheese is completely hot and melted.

Smoked Cheddar Boursin

LOMPOC CAFÉ, BAR HARBOR

makes 2 ½ cups

"At the Lompoc, this is a staple of our fall menu. We serve it warm with French bread, accompanied by plates of grapes, spiced nuts, and sliced pears and apples. You can use it as a spread for turkey, ham, or chicken sandwiches, too. Use it to make Smoked Cheddar Boursin Baked Chicken with Apple Chutney on the side (see Index)."

—CHEF LISE DESROCHERS

2 tablespoons chopped fresh parsley
1 tablespoon chopped fresh garlic
1 ½ teaspoons dried basil
½ teaspoon dried thyme
½ teaspoon freshly ground black pepper
8 ounces smoked Cheddar cheese, grated
12 ounces cream cheese, at room temperature

Put all the ingredients in the bowl of a food processor and pulse until smooth.

The bar at Lompoc Café

Seal Cove Goat Cheese Terrine

LOMPOC CAFÉ, BAR HARBOR

makes 12–15 slices

Barbara Brooks owns Seal Cove Farm, where she raises goats and produces a delicious, tangy goat cheese that is delivered to Lompoc Café fresh each week. This pretty terrine must be prepared the day before you plan to serve it. It's easy to put together and makes a colorful addition to a party buffet table.

⅓ cup prepared pesto (see Index)
⅓ cup softened sun-dried tomatoes, reconstituted or oil-packed
1 pound goat cheese

1. Place the pesto in a tea strainer and press lightly to extract most of the olive oil. Dry the sun-dried tomatoes between paper towels.
2. Divide the goat cheese into thirds. In a food processor, whip one-third of the goat cheese until smooth and spreadable. Remove to a small bowl, cover, and set aside. Next, in the food processor, combine one-third of the goat cheese with the pesto. Pulse until smooth and set aside. Clean and dry the food processor bowl and blade, then repeat the procedure with the remaining one-third of the goat cheese and the sun-dried tomatoes to make a smooth purée.
3. Line a small loaf pan, or other 1-quart dish or casserole, with 2 generous lengths of plastic wrap, letting the excess hang over the sides of the dish. Spread the sun-dried tomato mixture evenly over the bottom, filling all edges and corners. Carefully spread the plain goat cheese layer on top, smoothing the surface. Finish with the pesto mixture for the final layer.
4. Cover the surface of the terrine completely with the overhanging plastic wrap, pressing out any air pockets. Chill overnight.
5. To serve, pull away the plastic wrap from the top of the terrine, invert it onto a serving platter, then peel away the rest of the wrap. You can preslice the terrine using a knife dipped into warm water, or serve the terrine whole, garnished with fresh basil leaves. Serve with crackers or crostini.

Creative Coastal Cooking

Roasted Red Pepper and Goat Cheese Dip

MARKET ON MAIN, ROCKLAND

makes 2 cups

Here's a flavorful spread for sandwiches, crackers, or crostini. As a party buffet dip, this pairs nicely with Olivada Tapenade (see p. 34).

8 ounces fresh goat cheese
4 ounces cream cheese, room temperature
1 tablespoon fresh-squeezed lemon juice
2 tablespoons olive oil
2 tablespoons minced fresh basil, plus additional for garnish
½ cup finely chopped roasted red bell pepper (see Index)
a pinch of cayenne
salt and freshly ground black pepper to taste

In a food processor, pulse the goat cheese, cream cheese, lemon juice, olive oil, and basil until smooth. Scrape the mixture into a small mixing bowl and fold in the roasted pepper. Season to taste with cayenne, salt, and pepper. Serve drizzled with a little additional olive oil and chopped basil.

Frances Holdgate in MOM's kitchen

Kerry's Olivada Tapenade

CAFÉ MIRANDA, ROCKLAND

serves 4–6 as an appetizer

Garlicky tapenade comes from Provence. It's a spread you can serve in a bowl at parties, along with some sturdy crackers or crusty bread, or on individual plates as a dressed-up first course. You can use just about any type of olive in this recipe.

Rule of thumb: If you like the way an olive tastes on its own, you'll love it in tapenade.

7 ounces good-quality pitted olives, black or green (see Note)
5 large fresh basil leaves
3 cloves garlic, peeled
½ cup extra-virgin olive oil
2 tablespoons water

Toss all the ingredients together in a bowl, then process (or blend) in batches. You can purée the tapenade until it's completely smooth, or pulse the mixture to a somewhat coarser texture, if desired.

Serve the tapenade with julienne strips of roasted red pepper, thick slices of fresh mozzarella cheese, lemon wedges, and slices of crusty European-style bread.

Note: Kerry Altiero prefers dry, oil-cured French olives for this recipe. If you use olives that are packed in jars or brine, be sure to rinse and drain them thoroughly before making the tapenade.

Artichoke Dip

MARKET ON MAIN, ROCKLAND

makes about 5 cups

Serve this dip chilled, or bake it in a small casserole until hot and bubbly, then serve with crackers or crostini. It's also a good spread for a ham-and-cheese sandwich.

2 cups drained water-packed artichoke hearts
8 ounces cream cheese, at room temperature
⅔ cup sour cream
½ teaspoon minced fresh garlic
2 tablespoons fresh-squeezed lemon juice
2 tablespoons olive oil
⅔ cup shredded Pecorino Romano cheese
1 ½ cups grated Cheddar cheese
¼ teaspoon cayenne, or more to taste
¼ cup minced fresh flat-leaf parsley
⅓ cup chopped scallions
salt and freshly ground black pepper to taste

1. Remove any tough, stalky leaves from the artichokes. Pat them dry between paper towels, coarsely chop them, and set them aside.
2. Place the cream cheese, sour cream, garlic, lemon juice, and olive oil in the bowl of a food processor. Pulse until smooth.
3. Add the cheeses and cayenne and pulse a few times to blend.
4. Add the artichokes and remaining ingredients and pulse until the dip is spreadable, but still a bit chunky. Season to taste with salt and pepper.

Miranda's Mediterranean Baked Croutons

CAFÉ MIRANDA, ROCKLAND

serves 4 as an appetizer or luncheon entrée

Juicy and hot, these "croutons" come out of the oven dripping with strong flavors. They are really big chunks of focaccia bread, baked with a topping of tomato, peppers, tuna, and artichokes. At Café Miranda, Kerry Altiero "ages" the topping for a day or two in the refrigerator so the flavors can meld. A big, rustic red wine is what you'll need, and maybe a little grated Parmesan.

2 Roma tomatoes, seeded and diced
1 can (14–16 ounces) artichoke hearts, drained and coarsely chopped
6 whole, jarred pepperoncini peppers
3 tablespoons juice from pepperoncini
½ cup finely chopped fennel tops (the feathery green tops)
1 can (6 ounces) Italian-style tuna packed in olive oil, or water-packed tuna,
     well drained
¼ cup diced onion
2 cloves garlic, minced
1 cup chopped roasted red pepper (see Index)
½ cup extra-virgin olive oil
¼ cup pitted oil-cured black olives (Sicilian, if you can find them)
salt and freshly ground black pepper to taste
1 cup packed fresh spinach leaves
1 tablespoon torn fresh herbs, such as basil or oregano
a loaf of fresh focaccia, split lengthwise and cut into approximately
     3-inch-square slabs

1. Toss all the ingredients, except the focaccia, together in a mixing bowl. Do this at least 1 day in advance. Cover and refrigerate until you are ready to assemble and serve the dish.
2. Preheat the oven to 400°F. Layer the bread slabs in a 9 x 13-inch glass baking dish. Spoon the topping, including all the juices, over the bread. Bake for about 25 minutes, or until the vegetables begin to brown and caramelize.
3. Serve the croutons on plates with pan juices spooned on top.

Variations on Miranda's Mediterranean Baked Croutons

For the tuna you can substitute 1 cup of any of the following ingredients, or use a combination:
- Smoked mozzarella cut into ½-inch cubes
- Slices of buffalo mozzarella
- Feta cheese chunks
- Diced pepperoni
- Sliced mushrooms

Baked Spinach Ball Hors d'Oeuvres

BURNING TREE, BAR HARBOR

makes about 40 spinach balls

¼ cup olive oil
1 cup minced onion
1 teaspoon minced fresh garlic
20 ounces fresh spinach leaves, well rinsed and dried
2 cups fine fresh bread crumbs
4 eggs, beaten
½ cup finely grated Parmesan cheese
½ cup (1 stick) melted butter

1. Heat the olive oil in a large skillet and sauté the onion and garlic over low heat until soft. Set aside to cool.
2. Place the spinach in a large pot with 2 tablespoons of water. Cover and steam briefly, just until the spinach wilts. Place the spinach in a colander to drain. When it's cool enough to handle, squeeze out any excess water, then finely chop.
3. Place the onion-garlic mixture, spinach, and all the remaining ingredients in a mixing bowl and stir to combine. Roll the mixture into bite-sized balls and place them on a platter. Cover and refrigerate for 1 hour.
4. Preheat the oven to 375°F. Line a baking sheet with waxed or parchment paper and arrange the balls on the sheet. Bake for 20 minutes. Serve while still warm.

Carpaccio à la Coturri

CAFÉ MIRANDA, ROCKLAND

serves 2–3 as an appetizer

"This one was done for a wine-and-food-pairing event at Café Miranda with California vintner Tony Coturri of H. Coturri & Sons of Sonoma. It was an over-the-top experience in every way. Of course, if you can find it, you should get a Coturri Founder's Series Red to accompany this dish. Prepare to have your socks blown off to the next county! This has more steps and ingredients than some recipes, but it's worth it. This batch serves two or three as an appetizer, but is easily expandable to serve a big gathering."
—KERRY ALTIERO, CHEF-OWNER, CAFÉ MIRANDA

You can sear the filet mignon over very hot coals or quick-smoke it at about 350°F in a smoker. The trick is cooking it no further than rare to medium rare, then allowing it to cool before you slice it so that it will retain its juices. You can prep the meat a day in advance, since carpaccio is traditionally served chilled or at room temperature. Be sure to soak the currants in the vinegar overnight. When you are ready to serve the dish, have handy a very sharp knife and a big platter for serving.

1 clove garlic
¼ cup vegetable oil
1 filet mignon (about 6 ounces)
1 tablespoon dried currants, soaked overnight in 1 tablespoon good
  balsamic vinegar
a pinch of salt
1 teaspoon freshly ground black pepper
1 tablespoon snipped fresh chives
2 tablespoons chopped fresh Italian parsley
2–3 tablespoons extra-virgin olive oil
1 tablespoon large capers, drained

1. Purée the garlic with the vegetable oil and toss it into a plastic food bag with the steak. Push the air out of the bag and seal it so the steak is covered with the marinade. Let sit at room temperature for 1 hour, or overnight in the refrigerator.
2. Grill the steak to medium rare—an internal temperature of 140°F.
3. Let the steak cool. You can prepare the carpaccio right away, or chill the beef, if you prefer.
4. Hold the filet on its side and slice against the grain as thinly as you can. Fan the slices in a single layer over the platter.
5. Sprinkle the currants and vinegar over the beef. Season with salt and pepper, then garnish with the capers and chopped parsley. Serve with red wine and a crusty loaf of bread.

Creative Coastal Cooking

Sautéed Shrimp in Extra-Hot Mojo Sauce

CAFÉ THIS WAY, BAR HARBOR

serves 4 as an appetizer

It's the seeds and veins inside the jalapeño pepper that emit most of the heat. Chef Julie Harris at Café This Way uses whole jalapeños in this recipe, so go easy on the Mojo Sauce with your first bite or two. Then throw caution to the wind. Just have a bottle of ice-cold beer at the ready.

Serve Mojo Sauce on the side with things like grilled or fried seafood and poultry. Douse your eggs and omelets with it, too.

8 fresh jalapeño peppers
8 cloves garlic
1 tablespoon ground cumin
2 bay leaves
1 teaspoon red wine vinegar
1 cup good-quality olive oil
2 tablespoons vegetable oil
1 pound large fresh shrimp, peeled and deveined

1. Remove the stems from the jalapeño peppers, then chop them coarsely, retaining the seeds.
2. Place the peppers in the bowl of a food processor or blender. Add the garlic, cumin, bay leaves, and vinegar. Process the mixture to a purée. With the motor running, slowly drizzle in the olive oil. The mixture should thicken to make a saucy dip. Refrigerate immediately to prevent separation.
3. Just before serving, heat the vegetable oil in a large skillet. When the oil is very hot, add the shrimp all at once and toss for 2 minutes, or until the shrimp are pink and cooked through. Serve immediately with Mojo Sauce on the side for dipping.

Chile Pepper How-to

Always be careful when handling fresh hot peppers and wash up quickly after you've chopped them. Remember that when they are puréed, they can give off a stinging vapor that can burn your eyes. Just work fast and stand back!

Grilled Sea Scallops Dressed in Mustard and Lemon

CAFÉ MIRANDA, ROCKLAND

serves 2 as an appetizer

Here's Kerry Altiero's quick and tangy recipe for big, sweet sea scallops. Slivers of fennel freshen this dish with an aniselike taste, always a great flavor match with shellfish. Serve with rice and a dry white wine.

This dish works best when the scallops are cooked on a sizzling charcoal grill, but an indoor grill also works, as long as it's hot enough to leave those tasty grill marks on the scallops.

8 ounces large sea scallops, any tough connective bits trimmed away
2 tablespoons vegetable oil
1 small fresh fennel bulb
¼ cup snipped fresh chives
juice of 1 lemon
2 teaspoons prepared whole-grain mustard (any good-quality brand, but Kerry prefers Plochman's)
¼ cup extra-virgin olive oil
a pinch of salt and a generous grinding of fresh black pepper

1. Toss the scallops in the vegetable oil and set aside. Fire up the grill until the coals are very hot.
2. Trim the feathery green tops from the fennel bulb, then slice the bulb in half from top to bottom. Remove the hard core, then place the bulb cut-side down on a cutting board. With a very sharp knife, slice the fennel against the grain as thinly as possible. This can also be done on a mandoline slicer, if you have one.
3. In a serving bowl, toss together the fennel, chives, lemon juice, mustard, olive oil, salt, and pepper.
4. Grill the scallops: A fresh scallop needs just a minute or two per side of grilling time. As the scallops are done, lift them off the grill and into the bowl with the other ingredients. Gently toss the scallops in the dressing and serve.

Kerry Altiero at his wood-fired oven at Café Miranda

Fresh Crabmeat Sauté

STREET & CO., PORTLAND

serves 2 as an appetizer

This simple dish of few ingredients serves as a conveyance for sweet, fresh crab. Chef Abby Harmon serves it with a cold glass of Chardonnay. You can convert this into a main course by mounding it on top of a bowl of steaming risotto, topped with plenty of grated Parmesan.

¼ cup (½ stick) unsalted butter
½ cup sliced button mushrooms
6 ounces fresh crabmeat, picked over for shell bits
2 cups fresh watercress leaves, loosely packed
salt and freshly ground pepper to taste
Parmesan croutons (see Note)

1. Melt the butter in a skillet and continue heating until it just begins to brown.
2. Add the mushrooms and crabmeat and toss until the mushrooms begin to soften. Add the watercress and continue to toss until it is wilted and tender, just a minute or two longer.
3. Season the mixture to taste with salt and pepper and serve immediately, mounded on top of the Parmesan croutons with pan juices poured over the top.

Note: To make Parmesan croutons, cut a loaf of very crusty European-style bread into thick slices. Butter the bread lightly and dust with grated Parmesan cheese. Broil until golden brown.

Island Crab Cakes

THOMASTON CAFÉ, THOMASTON

makes 6 cakes

This simple recipe won't overwhelm the sweet crabmeat. Serve with lemon wedges and Lemon-Caper Tartar Sauce (see Index).

2 tablespoons mayonnaise
1 tablespoon prepared Dijon mustard
1 tablespoon fresh-squeezed lemon juice
1 cup very fine fresh bread crumbs
1 pound fresh crabmeat, picked over for shells
cooking oil, for frying (canola or other light vegetable oil)

1. In a mixing bowl, stir together the mayonnaise, mustard, lemon juice, and bread crumbs. Add the crabmeat and toss gently with the other ingredients until just blended.
2. Divide the mixture into 6 equal portions, and shape each into a little cake. Cover and refrigerate until ready to fry.
3. Heat a sauté pan or a griddle and, using as little oil as possible, sauté the crab cakes until golden brown, about 3 minutes per side.

Lobster Quesadillas

LOMPOC CAFÉ, BAR HARBOR

You've got no lobster? Substitute almost any precooked meat and you'll still end up with a great-tasting quesadilla. Use grilled or barbecued chicken, shrimp, beef, or chorizo sausage.

For each quesadilla, you will need:

⅓ cup grated mild cheese, such as Monterey Jack, mozzarella, or Muenster
2 ounces chunk fresh lobster meat
¼ cup caramelized onions (see Index)
6 mushrooms, sliced and sautéed in a bit of butter
a few ripe avocado slices
1 tablespoon chopped scallions
1 large flour tortilla
vegetable oil, for frying

Heat a large skillet or griddle over medium-high heat until extremely hot. Starting with the cheese, layer all the ingredients on one half of the tortilla, then fold and brush the tortilla lightly with vegetable oil. Cook until brown on the first side, then flip and brown the second side. Serve with salsa and sour cream.

Bay Scallop Seviche

CHERIE'S, KENNEBUNK

serves 6

The acidic citrus juices "cook" the scallops as they marinate in this classic seviche. Serve over a bed of greens as a salad course or luncheon entrée.

1 pound very fresh bay scallops
1 cup fresh-squeezed orange juice
½ cup fresh-squeezed lime juice
1 teaspoon minced fresh garlic
½ cup slivered red onion
2 fresh jalapeño peppers, seeded and minced
2 ripe tomatoes, seeded and diced
1 cup prepared ketchup
1 tablespoon minced fresh cilantro
½ teaspoon dried oregano
3 tablespoons extra-virgin olive oil
salt and freshly ground black pepper to taste

1. Toss the scallops with the orange and lime juices. Cover and refrigerate for 1 hour.
2. Add the remaining ingredients, cover, and refrigerate for at least 6 hours or overnight before serving.

Pan-Roasted Damariscotta River Oysters

PRIMO, ROCKLAND

serves 4

Chef Melissa Kelly recommends a good bottle of champagne with this special dish. You can serve the oysters in their shells as Melissa does at Primo, or simply spoon them into small gratin dishes to serve.

1 tablespoon olive oil
4 ounces tasso ham, cut into thin julienne strips
¼ cup chopped scallions, white part only
1 clove minced fresh garlic
12 plump shucked oysters, liquor (about ¼ cup) and scrubbed empty
    shells reserved
1 cup heavy cream
4 ounces crawfish tails, shelled (optional)
¼ cup chopped scallion green tops
salt, freshly ground black pepper, and Tabasco to taste

1. Heat the olive oil in a medium skillet. Add the tasso and sauté briefly. Add the scallion whites and garlic and cook until translucent, 2 or 3 minutes.
2. Add the oysters and their liquor. Bring to a boil, then add the cream with a pinch of black pepper and simmer, uncovered, until reduced by half.
3. Add the crawfish tails and scallion greens and heat through. Season to taste with salt, Tabasco, and additional pepper.
4. To serve, briefly warm the reserved oyster shells in the oven, then spoon the mixture back into them. Serve immediately.

Mussels in Ginger Wheat Ale

LOMPOC CAFÉ, BAR HARBOR

serves 4 as an appetizer

Make no mistake, the ale used in this dish is of the alcoholic variety—not the sweet stuff! Serve with plenty of warm, crusty bread to sop up the broth.

½ cup (1 stick) butter
2 bottles (12 ounces each) good ale or beer, preferably a ginger-flavored
    brew such as the Lompoc Café's own Ginger Wheat Ale
6 thin slices ("coins") peeled fresh gingerroot
2 teaspoons minced fresh garlic
2 pounds live mussels, scrubbed and debearded (see Index)
¼ cup chopped scallions

Place the butter, ale, gingerroot, and garlic in a large stockpot with a tight-fitting lid. Bring to a full boil. Add the mussels to the pot, cover, and steam for about 5 minutes, until all the shells have opened. To serve, pour the mussels and all into a large serving bowl, or individual soup or pasta bowls. Garnish with the chopped scallions.

Mussels Steamed in Saffron Cream

LOCAL 188

serves 4 as an appetizer (2 as a main course)

2 pounds live mussels
½ cup dry white wine
1 teaspoon saffron threads, crushed
1 cup heavy or whipping cream
4 fresh or canned plum tomatoes, seeded and chopped
1 tablespoon minced fresh garlic
½ cup vegetable or chicken stock (see Index)

1. Scrub the mussels and place them in a pan of very cold water.
2. In a small saucepan, combine the wine and saffron. Simmer until reduced by half. Add the cream and reduce by one-third. Set aside.
3. Drain the mussels in a colander and pull off any beards. In a skillet or Dutch oven large enough to hold all the mussels, heat the tomatoes, garlic, and stock. Add the reserved saffron cream and the mussels to the pan and bring to a boil over high heat. Cover and cook until the mussels have opened, about 4 to 6 minutes.
4. Serve the mussels in the shell with plenty of the pan juices ladled over them.

Chapter 2
Soup Pot Luck
CHILLED AND HOT, CHOWDERS AND BISQUES

The kitchen, Street & Co.

Creative Coastal Cooking

Cold Cucumber and Avocado Soup

LOMPOC CAFÉ, BAR HARBOR

serves 8

2 ripe avocados (halved, pitted, and flesh scooped out), plus additional
    avocado for garnish (optional)
¼ cup chopped scallions
5 cups diced peeled cucumbers (English or "hothouse" variety)
¼ cup chopped flat-leaf parsley
2 tablespoons minced fresh cilantro, plus extra for garnish
1 teaspoon finely minced garlic
2 cups plain yogurt
½ cup cream
½ cup cold water
½ teaspoon salt
¼ teaspoon freshly ground black pepper
½ teaspoon ground cumin
2 teaspoons fresh-squeezed lime juice
chopped ripe tomatoes, for garnish (optional)

Place all the ingredients in the bowl of a food processor and purée until very
smooth. Put the soup in a bowl, then cover with plastic wrap, pressing the wrap
directly over the surface of the soup to keep it from discoloring. Use additional
plastic wrap to be sure the soup is completely covered as it chills in the
refrigerator, at least 1 hour.

    Garnish the soup with cilantro, ripe chopped tomatoes in season, and
additional avocado sliced just before serving.

Chilled Zucchini Soup

CHERIE'S, KENNEBUNK

serves 6

2 tablespoons olive oil
½ cup thinly sliced scallions
4 cups chopped zucchini
2 cups chicken stock (see Index)
½ teaspoon dried rosemary
1 cup cream
1 tablespoon fresh-squeezed lemon juice
salt and white pepper to taste
snipped fresh chives, for garnish

1. Heat the olive oil in a saucepan. Add the scallions and zucchini and sauté for 5 minutes.
2. Add the stock, rosemary, and cream and simmer, uncovered, until the vegetables are tender. Cool the soup to room temperature.
3. Purée the soup in a blender or food processor. Season with lemon juice, salt, and white pepper to taste. Cover and refrigerate until very cold. Serve garnished with snipped chives.

Summer Berry Soup

THOMASTON CAFÉ, THOMASTON

serves 4–6

1 pint (2 cups) fresh or frozen raspberries
2 cups peeled, sliced peaches
½ cup sugar
2 cups fresh-squeezed orange juice
a pinch of ground cinnamon
¼ sour cream (optional)

Put the berries, peaches, and sugar into a blender or food processor. With the motor running, add the orange juice gradually until the soup is smooth. Stir in the cinnamon. Serve in chilled glasses or bowls with a dab of sour cream, if desired, and garnish with a sprig of fresh mint.

Summer Tomato Gazpacho

PRIMO, ROCKLAND

serves 12

Use your very best ripe and sweet summer tomatoes for gazpacho.

3 pounds overripe tomatoes, seeded and finely chopped
2 cups cubed stale bread (good-quality levain or sourdough, crusts removed)
1 each red, yellow, and green bell peppers, seeded and finely chopped
1 cup diced red onion
1 large English "hothouse" cucumber, finely chopped
2 fresh jalapeño peppers, seeded and minced
1 can (46 ounces) tomato juice
1 teaspoon ground cumin
1 teaspoon ground coriander
½ teaspoon chili powder
salt and freshly ground black pepper to taste
juice of 2 limes
½ cup sherry vinegar
½ cup extra-virgin olive oil
green Tabasco sauce to taste
sour cream and finely diced jicama, for garnish

Mix all the ingredients together in a large bowl and adjust the seasonings to taste. Serve well chilled, garnished with a dollop of sour cream and a spoonful of diced jicama.

Creamy Scallop and Crabmeat Chowder

STREET & CO., PORTLAND

serves 4–6

You can use scallops alone in this chowder, or add crabmeat to make a very special first course.

In this recipe chef Abby Harmon layers on the delicious anise flavors of fresh fennel, ground fennel seeds, and Pernod, the famous French apéritif. Pernod is used in the seafood dishes of New Orleans and has been manufactured in France for more than two hundred years. It's called pastis in the south of France, which translates roughly to "mixed up." Pernod, or pastis, is mixed with cold water to produce a sweet, licorice-flavored before-dinner drink to whet the appetite.

2 tablespoons vegetable oil
1 cup diced Spanish or yellow onion
1 carrot, peeled and diced
1 cup shaved fresh fennel bulb
2 teaspoons minced fresh garlic
1 ½ teaspoons ground fennel seeds
½ teaspoon ground white pepper (substitute black pepper, if you prefer)
1 cup dry white wine
¼ cup Pernod
3 cups fish stock (see Index)
1 medium russet potato, peeled and diced
2 tablespoons soft butter blended with 2 tablespoons flour
1 pound scallops
8 ounces Deer Isle crabmeat (optional)
2 cups heavy cream
salt to taste

1. Heat the vegetable oil in a soup pot. Add the onion, carrot, fresh fennel, and garlic and sauté until soft, about 5 to 7 minutes. Add the ground fennel seeds, pepper, wine, and Pernod. Stir and simmer, uncovered, for 3 minutes.
2. Add the fish stock and the diced potato and continue to simmer for about 10 minutes, until the potato is tender.
3. Whisk in the butter-flour mixture and stir the simmering soup until it begins to thicken, about 5 minutes.
4. Add the scallops (and optional crabmeat) along with the cream. Stir gently to combine. Simmer, uncovered, until the scallops are cooked, about 5 minutes. Season to taste with salt, if needed.

Haddock Chowder

THOMASTON CAFÉ, THOMASTON

serves 8–10

Here's the basic recipe for traditional fish chowder. Use haddock, cod, sole, bass, salmon, or a combination. Strong, oily fish such as bluefish or tuna are, as a rule, not used in cream-based chowders, but in brothy, tomato-based versions.

The better the stock, the better the soup. If you have a good, scratch-made fish stock, use it. If not, buy a tub of fish stock base, such as Minor's brand, and keep it on hand. Bottled clam juice is also an acceptable substitute.

½ cup (1 stick) unsalted butter
1 cup diced onion
4 cups peeled, diced potatoes
8 cups fish stock (see Index) or prepared clam juice
2 tablespoons chopped fresh thyme leaves, or 1 tablespoon dried
2 pounds haddock fillet, all skin and bones removed
4 cups heavy or whipping cream
salt and pepper to taste

1. Melt the butter in a soup pot, add the onion, and cook until soft, about 10 minutes.
2. Add the potatoes and the stock or clam juice. Bring to a simmer and cook just until the potatoes are tender but still firm.
3. Add the thyme and the whole haddock fillet and return to a simmer. As the fish cooks in the hot stock, it will begin to break up into bite-sized pieces as you gently stir the chowder.
4. When the haddock is fully cooked, add the cream and stir gently over low heat until the chowder is hot. Do not boil. Season to taste with salt and pepper.

Thomaston Harbor

Italian Mussel Soup

THOMASTON CAFÉ, THOMASTON

serves 4–6

2 pounds live mussels
2 tablespoons olive oil
1 cup chopped onion
1 tablespoon minced fresh garlic
2 cups dry white wine
1 whole bay leaf
2 tablespoons chopped fresh basil, or 1 tablespoon dried
2 pounds fresh ripe tomatoes, seeded and diced, or 1 can (28 ounces) crushed
   plum tomatoes, with juices
1 tablespoon ground cumin
1 teaspoon Tabasco, or more to taste
salt and freshly ground black pepper to taste

1. Scrub the mussels under cold running water and pull away any "beards."
   Discard any open or cracked ones.
2. In a large (non-aluminum) pot, heat the olive oil and sauté the onion and
   garlic for 5 minutes. Add the wine, bay leaf, and mussels and bring the pot to
   a boil. Cover and cook for 7 minutes, or until the mussel shells have opened.
3. Remove the mussels (and any empty shells) from the pot. Discard the shells,
   and set the cooked mussels aside while you finish the soup.
4. Add the basil, tomatoes, and seasonings to the pot and simmer, uncovered,
   until the tomatoes are soft, about 15 to 20 minutes. Remove the bay leaf.
5. Return the mussels to the soup pot, season to taste, and serve.

Thomaston Harbor

Tomato-Cheddar Soup

MARKET ON MAIN, ROCKLAND

serves 8

½ cup olive oil
½ cup (1 stick) butter
2 cups chopped onion
2 stalks celery, chopped
1 carrot, peeled and sliced
1 tablespoon minced fresh garlic
¼ cup chopped fresh basil, or 1 tablespoon dried
½ teaspoon red pepper flakes
8 cups whole canned tomatoes in their juices
1 cup dry white wine
2 cups water or chicken stock (see Index)
1 cup heavy cream
2 cups grated sharp white Cheddar cheese
salt and freshly ground black pepper to taste

1. Heat the olive oil in a soup pot. Add the butter, onion, celery, carrot, and garlic. Cook over low heat until the vegetables are soft, about 10 minutes.
2. Add the basil, pepper flakes, tomatoes, wine, and water or stock. Bring to a simmer and cook, uncovered, for 30 minutes.
3. Purée the soup with a handheld immersion blender, or in batches in a regular blender or food processor.
4. Add the cream and grated cheese to the hot soup and stir until smooth (do not boil). Season to taste with salt and pepper.

Creamy Tomato Herb Soup with Pesto Cream

LOMPOC CAFÉ, BAR HARBOR

serves 6–8

"On damp, rainy days all of Bar Harbor's visiting campers decide to crowd into town and wait out the storm while having a beer and some hot soup. This is our 'Yikes!—we're almost out of soup' solution. If you hustle, this soup can be ready in less than an hour."

—CHEF LISE DESROCHERS

2 tablespoons olive oil
¾ cup diced onion
¼ cup diced celery
1 teaspoon minced garlic
½ teaspoon dried oregano
¼ teaspoon dried thyme
¼ teaspoon dried rosemary
2 tablespoons chopped fresh basil, or 1 tablespoon dried
4 ½ cups canned crushed tomatoes
1 ½ cups good chicken or vegetable stock (see Index)
3–4 teaspoons sugar
½ cup heavy or whipping cream
salt and freshly ground black pepper to taste

For the Pesto Cream:

½ cup sour cream
½ cup heavy or whipping cream
2 tablespoons prepared Basil-Arugula Pesto (see Index)

1. Heat the olive oil in a soup pot over medium heat. Sauté the onion, celery, and garlic for 5 minutes. Add the herbs and cook for 5 minutes more, or until the vegetables are soft.
2. Add the tomatoes, stock, and 2 teaspoons of the sugar. Bring the soup to a boil, reduce the heat, and simmer, uncovered, for 30 minutes.
3. Prepare the Pesto Cream: Place all the ingredients in a small mixing bowl and whisk until thick and smooth. Cover and refrigerate.
4. Stir the 1/2 cup heavy cream into the simmering soup. Season to taste with salt and pepper, and an additional teaspoon or two of sugar if the soup seems too tart or acidic.
5. To serve, ladle the soup into bowls and top each with a dollop of the Pesto Cream.

Cheddar and Ale Soup

LOMPOC CAFÉ, BAR HARBOR

makes 10 cups

At the Lompoc Lise Desrochers and Pattie Savoie make this soup with Bar Harbor Real Ale, but any really good microbrewed nut-brown ale will do. Remember to be patient, says Lise, when you add the cheese a little at time—"or you'll end up with a giant congealed lump of cheese at the bottom of your soup pot. I speak from experience, believe me!"

2 tablespoons butter
1 ½ cups diced onion
1 cup diced celery
1 cup diced carrot
1 teaspoon minced garlic
5 cups good chicken or vegetable stock (see Index)
2 cups nut-brown ale
12 ounces extra-sharp Cheddar cheese, grated
½ cup flour
1 cup heavy or whipping cream
¾ teaspoon salt, or more to taste
freshly ground black pepper

1. Heat the butter in a soup pot over medium heat. Sauté the onion, celery, carrot, and garlic for about 10 minutes. Add the stock and the ale, stir, and simmer for 15 minutes, or until the vegetables are very tender.
2. In a large plastic or paper bag, toss together the grated cheese and the flour until combined, the cheese evenly coated with flour.
3. As the soup simmers, add the cheese-flour mixture by small handfuls, whisking constantly. Be sure the cheese is completely melted before adding each additional handful.
4. Once all the cheese-flour mixture has been incorporated into the soup, whisk in the cream and season to taste with salt and pepper.

Note: If you need to reheat this soup, do so gently over low heat so that it won't burn or separate.

Five-Onion Sweet Potato Bisque

LOMPOC CAFÉ, BAR HARBOR

serves 12

A rich cream soup, with lightly caramelized sweet onions and a touch of sherry.

6 cups peeled and cubed sweet potatoes
6 cups good chicken or vegetable stock (see Index)
2 cups thinly sliced Spanish or yellow onion, any "sweet" variety
1 cup thinly sliced red onion
1 ½ cups chopped scallions, plus extra for garnish
2 tablespoons minced garlic
1 ½ cups thinly sliced leeks (white part only)
4 tablespoons olive oil
1 ½ cups heavy or whipping cream
¼ cup dry sherry
salt and freshly ground black pepper to taste

1. In a soup pot, simmer the potatoes in the stock until they are tender. Cool the mixture a bit, then purée it in batches in a blender or food processor, returning the mixture to the soup pot.
2. Preheat the oven to 450°F. In a large roasting pan, toss the yellow and red onions with 2 tablespoons of the olive oil. Bake the onions, stirring often, until they are soft and begin to brown around the edges, about 20 minutes. Lift the cooked onions from the pan and reserve. Add the remaining oil to the roasting pan along with the scallions, garlic, and leeks. Stir, then roast until browned, about 10 minutes.
3. Add all the roasted vegetables to the soup pot and heat slowly over low heat. Finish with the cream, sherry, and salt and pepper to taste. Garnish each bowl with chopped scallions.

Sweet Potato and Apple Bisque

CHERIE'S, KENNEBUNK

serves 8–10

¼ cup (½ stick) butter
½ cup chopped onion
1 carrot, peeled and chopped
2 stalks celery, chopped
3 sweet potatoes, peeled and chopped
3 Granny Smith apples, peeled, cored, and chopped
½ cup white wine
4 cups rich chicken stock (see Index)
2 bay leaves
3 sage leaves
1 ½ teaspoons dried thyme
2 cups heavy cream
¼ teaspoon ground nutmeg
salt and white pepper to taste

1. Melt the butter in a soup pot. Add the onion, carrot, celery, sweet potatoes, and apples and sauté over low heat until the vegetables begin to soften, about 10 minutes.
2. Add the wine, stock, and herbs and simmer, uncovered, for 15 to 20 minutes, until the vegetables are tender.
3. Remove the bay and sage leaves from the pot, then purée the soup in batches in a blender or food processor.
4. Return the purée to the soup pot, stir in the cream and nutmeg, and heat the soup. Season to taste with salt and white pepper.

Sherried Lentil Soup

LOMPOC CAFÉ, BAR HARBOR

serves 8

1 tablespoon olive oil
1 cup diced onion
¾ cup diced celery
¾ cup diced carrot
1 ½ teaspoons minced garlic
1 teaspoon dried thyme
1 teaspoon dried basil
½ teaspoon dried oregano
1 teaspoon black pepper
1 ¼ cups dried brown lentils
¼ cup white pearl barley
6 cups vegetable or chicken stock (see Index)
2 tablespoons soy sauce
¼ cup dry sherry
¼ cup minced parsley

1. Heat the oil in a soup pot. Add the onion, celery, carrot, and garlic and cook for about 5 minutes, until the onion is soft. Add the herbs and pepper and cook for 5 minutes more.
2. Add the lentils, barley, stock, and soy sauce and bring to a boil. Reduce the heat and simmer, partially covered, for about 1 ½ hours.
3. Add the sherry and parsley and simmer for another 20 to 30 minutes, or until the lentils and barley are soft.

Stewed French Lentils

CHERIE'S, KENNEBUNK

serves 6–8

2 tablespoons olive oil
3 large leeks (white part and 1 inch green), trimmed, rinsed, and finely diced
1 ½ cups finely diced celery
1 cup finely diced onion
2 carrots, peeled and diced
8 ounces small French lentils
8 cups rich chicken stock (see Index)
3 bay leaves
4 whole sprigs fresh thyme
salt and freshly ground black pepper to taste

1. Heat the olive oil in a soup pot. Sauté the vegetables until they begin to soften, about 10 minutes.
2. Add the lentils and toss with the vegetables. Add the stock and herbs.
3. Simmer, uncovered, until the lentils are just tender, 20 to 30 minutes.
4. Remove the bay leaves and thyme sprigs. Season to taste with salt and pepper and serve.

Creamy New Potato and Sweet Corn Chowder

CHERIE'S, KENNEBUNK

serves 4–6

½ cup (1 stick) butter, softened
¾ cup finely chopped Spanish onion
1 pound unpeeled small new potatoes (redskins), scrubbed and cubed
1 ½ cups chicken stock, canned or scratch-made (see Index)
1 can (14 ounces) cream-style corn
2 cups corn kernels, cut fresh from the cob or frozen
1 cup heavy cream
1 cup half-and-half or whole milk
2 tablespoons flour
1 tablespoon snipped fresh dill, or 1 teaspoon dried
½ teaspoon salt
¼ teaspoon white pepper

1. Melt half the butter in a soup pot. Add the onion and cook over low heat, stirring, until soft, about 15 minutes (do not brown).
2. Add the cubed potatoes and the stock and bring to a boil. Simmer until the potatoes are tender but still firm.
3. Add the cream-style corn, the corn kernels, the cream, and the half-and-half. Bring to a simmer. Meanwhile, mix the remaining butter with the flour until smooth. Whisk the mixture into the soup and simmer for about 5 minutes more, until thick and creamy.
4. To serve, add the dill, salt, and white pepper to taste.

Chapter 3

Salads for All Seasons

MASTERING VINAIGRETTES, GREENS, GRAINS,
FRUITS, NUTS, AND MORE

Mastering Vinaigrettes

- Vinegars and mustards vary in their degree of tartness and sweetness—thus the ratio of acid to oil in a vinaigrette also varies. For very sharp vinegars, use 1 part vinegar to 4 parts oil; for milder or sweeter vinegars, use a 1:3 ratio.
- No vinaigrette is finished until you've tasted it to see how you like it.
- You can doctor any vinaigrette dressing with additional ingredients—acid or oil, garlic, salt, sugar, or honey—to achieve a result that pleases you.
- And not all vinaigrette dressings call for vinegar per se. You can make a delicious salad dressing using mustard alone. Look for mustards flavored with maple, cranberries, tarragon, horseradish, jalapeño peppers, and countless other ingredients.
- Vinaigrettes aren't just for salads. Use them as marinades and as sauces for seared or grilled fish and poultry—or marinate goat cheese or feta in vinaigrette before serving.

Balsamic Vinaigrette

MARKET ON MAIN, ROCKLAND

makes 2 cups

1 ½ teaspoons finely minced fresh garlic
1 tablespoon prepared Dijon mustard
½ teaspoon kosher salt
¼ teaspoon freshly ground black pepper
6 tablespoons aged balsamic vinegar—a good-quality, mellow balsamic
2 tablespoons honey, or more to taste
1 ½ cups extra-virgin olive oil

By hand:

In a small mixing bowl, whisk together all the ingredients—except the olive oil—and set aside for at least 30 minutes. When ready to dress the salad, slowly drizzle in the olive oil, whisking vigorously, to make a thick emulsion.

In a blender or food processor:

Place all the ingredients—except the olive oil—in the blender or food processor. Purée and set aside for 30 minutes. With the motor running, slowly drizzle in the olive oil.

Spicy Pesto Salad Croutons

COURTESY THE AUTHOR

makes 4 cups

½ cup (1 stick) butter
½ teaspoon All-Purpose Smoky Spice Blend (see Index)
2 tablespoons prepared Basil-Arugula Pesto (see Index), or any prepared
    basil pesto
1 teaspoon granulated garlic
½ teaspoon salt
½ loaf French bread, cut into 4 cups of ¾-inch cubes

1. Preheat the oven to 350°F.
2. In a saucepan, melt the butter and blend in the seasonings. Cook over low
   heat for 2 minutes.
3. In a large mixing bowl, drizzle the bread cubes with the butter mixture and
   toss until all the cubes are well coated.
4. Spread the cubes in one layer on a large baking sheet. Bake for 15 minutes,
   turning with a spatula every 5 minutes until the croutons are crisp and golden
   brown.
5. Remove the baking sheet from the oven and let the croutons cool completely
   before placing them in an airtight plastic bag.

Allison's Fresh Herb Vinaigrette

BURNING TREE, BAR HARBOR

makes 3 cups

4 cloves garlic
1 cup loosely packed fresh flat-leaf parsley
1 tablespoon snipped fresh dill
1 tablespoon snipped fresh chives
½ teaspoon celery seeds
2 tablespoons chopped fresh mint leaves
1 tablespoon honey
⅔ cup cider vinegar
½ teaspoon salt
¼ teaspoon freshly ground black pepper
1 cup olive oil
1 cup canola oil

Place all the ingredients—except the oils—in a food processor and purée. With the
motor running, slowly drizzle in the oils to make a thick emulsion.

Citrus Vinaigrette

BURNING TREE, BAR HARBOR

makes 3 cups

Try this vinaigrette on a green salad topped with grilled chicken or salmon. In the summer, when the corn comes in, Burning Tree uses it to dress Fresh Sweet Corn Salad (see below).

1 teaspoon minced fresh garlic
1 teaspoon salt
1 teaspoon sugar
1 ½ tablespoons finely grated orange zest
1 tablespoon grated fresh gingerroot
1 teaspoon dry mustard
½ cup fresh-squeezed lemon juice
¼ cup apple cider vinegar
2 cups canola oil

1. Place all the ingredients—except the canola oil—in a food processor or blender and purée.
2. With the motor running, drizzle in the oil to make a smooth emulsion. Store tightly covered in the refrigerator.

Fresh Sweet Corn Salad

BURNING TREE, BAR HARBOR

serves 4

6 ears sweet corn
1 cup diced red bell pepper
¼ cup minced red onion
¾ cup cherry tomatoes, cut in half
2 tablespoons chopped fresh basil leaves
½ cup Citrus Vinaigrette (see above), or more to taste
salt and freshly ground black pepper to taste

1. Plunge the sweet corn into boiling water for 3 minutes, remove to a colander, and rinse with cold tap water. Let the corn drain until the ears are cool enough to handle.
2. Slice the corn kernels from the cobs into a large salad bowl. Toss the corn with the remaining ingredients and season to taste. Serve chilled or at room temperature.

Ripe Tomato and Ricotta Salata Salad

BURNING TREE, BAR HARBOR

serves 4

For the smoked plum tomatoes:

Heat a few hardwood briquettes in a covered, outdoor charcoal grill. Add a layer of wet wood chips such as hickory, alder wood, or mesquite. Cut ripe plum tomatoes lengthwise and place them directly on the grill, skin-side down. Cover and let the tomatoes smoke at 200° to 250°F for about 45 minutes. When done, they will be soft and slightly charred, but still juicy.

For the Smoked Tomato Vinaigrette:

2 medium shallots, peeled
1 large clove garlic
3 smoked plum tomatoes (6 halves)
¼ cup red wine vinegar
½ teaspoon salt
½ teaspoon sugar
freshly ground black pepper to taste
¾ cup extra-virgin olive oil

1. Purée the shallots and garlic in a food processor. Add the smoked tomatoes, vinegar, salt, and sugar and pulse until nearly smooth.
2. With the motor running, drizzle in the olive oil to make a thick emulsion. Season to taste with pepper, and additional salt or sugar, if desired.

For the salad:

lettuce leaves or mixed greens for 4 salad plates
2 large very ripe summer tomatoes, thickly sliced
4 ounces Ricotta Salata cheese, shaved with a vegetable peeler into thin slices
8 leaves fresh basil, torn into small pieces

Smoked Tomato Vinaigrette

Arrange the lettuce or mixed greens on salad plates, then layer on the tomatoes, cheese, and basil. Drizzle on vinaigrette to taste. Serve with plenty of freshly ground black pepper.

Allison's French Green Beans and Feta Salad

BURNING TREE, BAR HARBOR

serves 4

1 pound young green beans (*haricots verts*), or substitute very fresh
    standard beans
1 small red onion, very thinly sliced
½ cup Walnut Oil Vinaigrette (see below)
¼ cup toasted chopped walnuts
¼ cup coarsely crumbled feta cheese
salt and freshly ground black pepper to taste

1. Steam the beans until just tender, about 4 minutes. Drain and rinse under cold water. Shake dry.
2. Toss the beans and onion with the vinaigrette and set aside to marinate for 1 hour.
3. To serve, toss in the walnuts and feta. Season to taste with a little salt, lots of pepper, and more vinaigrette, if needed.

Walnut Oil Vinaigrette

BURNING TREE, BAR HARBOR

makes 1 cup

This dressing is especially good on Field Greens Salad (see p. 67) topped with beets, or over arugula with a bit of sliced red onion, crumbled blue cheese, and toasted walnuts.

1 medium clove fresh garlic
1 small peeled shallot
1 teaspoon salt
1 teaspoon sugar
1 teaspoon dry mustard
⅓ cup white balsamic vinegar or other mild vinegar
1 cup walnut oil

Place all the ingredients—except the walnut oil—in the bowl of a food processor and pulse until smooth. With the motor running, slowly drizzle in the walnut oil to make a smooth emulsion.

Creative Coastal Cooking

Roasting Fresh Beets

1. Preheat the oven to 350°F. Rinse and dry the beets, trim the tops, and wrap each beet in foil.
2. Place the beets in a glass baking dish and bake for 45 minutes to 1 hour, or until fork-tender. Set aside until cool enough to handle.
3. Unwrap the beets over the baking dish to catch any juices. (Beet juice will stain sinks, countertops, and cutting boards.)
4. Slice or dice the beets. Cover and refrigerate until ready to use as part of a mixed salad.

Cherie's Field Greens Salad with Nuts, Roasted Pears, and Gorgonzola

CHERIE'S, KENNEBUNK

serves 6

A salad of many flavors and textures, this is an ideal first course for a holiday dinner, or any special meal. In addtion to the nuts and pears, Cherie Davis tops this salad with red grapes and crumbled Gorgonzola cheese. Finish the salad with a favorite dressing—balsamic, maple, or blueberry vinaigrettes are all good options (see Index).

For the field greens:

Soak 1 pound of fancy mixed field greens in plenty of very cold water for about 15 minutes. Drain and spin dry. Store the clean greens in the refrigerator, sealed in a plastic bag with a paper towel inside to absorb any excess water.

For the roasted pears:

    2 large ripe, firm pears
    1 tablespoon sugar
    1 tablespoon honey
    a pinch of cinnamon

1. Preheat the oven to 350°F. Line a baking sheet with foil. Spray the foil with nonstick cooking spray, or brush on a light coat of vegetable oil.
2. Core the pears and cut into 1/2-inch-thick slices. Toss the pears together with the sugar, honey, and cinnamon.
3. Spread the slices in a single layer on the baking sheet and bake, turning often, until they are beginning to soften and brown. Remove the pears from the oven and cool to room temperature. (Cover and refrigerate if you will be assembling the salad later.)

For the spiced nuts:

2 egg whites
¾ cup sugar
2 tablespoons paprika
2 teaspoons cayenne (or more to taste)
1 ½ teaspoons Worcestershire sauce
4 cups pecan halves
3 tablespoons melted butter (cooled)

1. Preheat the oven to 325°F. Line a baking sheet with foil. Spray the foil with nonstick cooking spray, or brush on a light coat of vegetable oil.
2. Beat the egg whites until they begin to foam. Add the sugar a little at a time and continue beating until the whites form stiff peaks. Blend in the spices and Worcestershire sauce, then fold in the pecans and the melted butter.
3. Spread the nuts in a single layer on the lined baking sheet. Bake for about 15 minutes, stirring often and watching closely so as not to burn the nuts. They are done when they begin to brown and the coating is crisp. Let cool completely.

To assemble the salad:

fancy mixed field greens
4 ounces Gorgonzola
1 cup red seedless grapes
roasted pears
spiced nuts
vinaigrette

Place a bed of greens on each individual salad plate. Top with the roasted pears and crumbled Gorgonzola; garnish with red seedless grapes and spiced nuts. Drizzle with vinaigrette.

Mixed Greens and Shiitake Salad with Warm Asian Dressing

Burning Tree, Bar Harbor

serves 4

The Asian dressing is heated before it's drizzled over this salad of sturdy greens. It can also be used chilled or at room temperature.

For the Asian Dressing:

makes 1 ½ cups

> 1 clove garlic
> 1 shallot
> 1 teaspoon sugar
> 1 tablespoon minced fresh gingerroot
> ⅓ cup rice wine vinegar or cider vinegar
> 1 teaspoon light miso paste (optional)
> 1 tablespoon dark toasted sesame seed oil
> 2 teaspoons tamari or soy sauce
> 1 cup canola oil

Place all the ingredients—except the canola oil—in a food processor and purée. With the motor running, slowly drizzle in the canola oil to make a thick emulsion.

For the salad:

serves 4

> 6 ounces mixed greens such as mizuna, Osaka purple, komatsuna, tat soi, spinach, or arugula
> 1 ruby red grapefruit
> 1 ripe avocado
> 1 tablespoon canola oil
> 8 fresh shiitake mushrooms, stemmed and thinly sliced
> ½ cup Asian Dressing, or more to taste

1. Make sure the greens are clean and dry. Divide them among 4 salad plates.
2. Peel the grapefruit and, with a sharp paring knife, trim the tough membranes away from the sections. Remove any seeds.
3. Peel and slice the avocado. Fan the grapefruit and avocado slices over the greens.
4. Heat the oil in a skillet and sauté the mushrooms over high heat until soft and lightly browned. Divide the mushrooms among the salads. Add the Asian Dressing to the skillet and heat. Drizzle the hot dressing over the salads and serve.

Salsa Verde Dressing

BURNING TREE, BAR HARBOR

makes about 1 ½ cups

This is a fresh-tasting dressing loaded with bright parsley and lemon flavors. At Burning Tree, Allison tosses it together with slivered red onion and tender steamed cauliflower served at room temperature. It can also be used to dress ripe tomatoes, pasta, green beans, or any seasonal vegetable dish.

½ cup pine nuts
2 cups packed fresh flat-leaf parsley, large stems removed
2 medium cloves fresh garlic
2 tablespoons capers, drained
¼ cup fresh-squeezed lemon juice
¾ cup extra-virgin olive oil
salt and freshly ground black pepper to taste

1. Place the pine nuts in a nonstick skillet and toss, over medium heat, until lightly browned. Remove the nuts from the pan to cool.
2. Place the pine nuts, parsley, garlic, capers, and lemon juice in a food processor and purée.
3. With the motor running, drizzle in the olive oil and process until smooth. Season the dressing to taste with salt and pepper.

Herbert's Eggless Caesar Dressing

THOMASTON CAFÉ

makes 2 cups

Here's a no-egg version of Caesar dressing that keeps well in the refrigerator.

1 large clove garlic
4 anchovy fillets, or more to taste
½ cup olive oil, plus 1 1/2 cups additional olive or canola oil
¼ cup cider vinegar
1 teaspoon prepared Dijon mustard
½ teaspoon salt
½ teaspoon ground white pepper
1 teaspoon sugar
¼ cup freshly grated Parmesan cheese

In a blender or food processor, purée the garlic and anchovy fillets in ½ cup of olive oil. Add the vinegar, mustard, salt, white pepper, and sugar. Pulse to blend. With the motor running, drizzle in the remaining 1 ½ cups of oil until thick. Add the grated cheese and pulse once again. Store in a glass container and shake well before using.

Et tu Brutes Caesar Salad

CAFÉ MIRANDA, ROCKLAND

makes 2 large salads, or 4 side salads

As Kerry Altiero says, his "Et tu Brutes" kills a Caesar. Don't fear the raw egg. In the fourteen years Café Miranda has offered this rich salad, they've never had a single problem with the free-range eggs they get from a Rockland-area farmer.

The traditional acid in a Caesar is fresh lemon juice, but it isn't added to the dressing in this version—lemon wedges are squeezed over the salad for a tangy finish.

For the dressing:

¾ cup freshly grated imported Romano or Parmesan cheese
1 egg, preferably organic
1 tablespoon water
1 teaspoon minced garlic
3 whole fresh basil leaves
¾ cup extra-virgin olive oil

1. Place the cheese, egg, water, garlic, and basil in a blender or food processor. Pulse until smooth.

2. With the motor running, slowly drizzle in the olive oil to make a thick, creamy dressing. Keep cold until ready to assemble the salad.

For the salad:

1 large head Romaine lettuce, torn, washed, chilled, and very dry
½ cup or more Spicy Pesto Salad Croutons (see Index)
slivered red onion to taste
½ cup julienne slices of roasted red pepper
12 or more anchovy fillets, drained of oil
1 whole lemon, cut into thick wedges
a grind of fresh black pepper

To assemble the salad:

In a large salad bowl, place the Romaine leaves, croutons, and red onion. Pour on the dressing and toss quickly. Arrange the salad on individual plates, then top with slices of roasted red pepper, anchovy fillets, lemon wedges, and coarsely ground black pepper.

Roasted Garlic and Buttermilk Salad Dressing

CAFÉ MIRANDA, ROCKLAND

makes 2 ½ cups

Kerry likes to use flavorful, sturdy greens such as curly endive, spinach, and radicchio under this dressing. Sometimes he tops the salad with crisp fried seafood like shrimp, clams, or scallops. In the summer, toss this dressing with cold pasta, then serve it over a bed of greens and top with ripe tomatoes and bacon bits for a Pasta BLT.

Use organic buttermilk if you can find it—the richer, the better.

Slow-roasted garlic is best for this dressing, but the quick-cook method works, too.

2 cups buttermilk
2 tablespoons good sherry vinegar
2 tablespoons puréed roasted garlic (see Index)
2 tablespoons extra-virgin olive oil
a scant pinch of salt and a grind of black pepper

Whip all the ingredients in a blender of food processor until smooth.

Roasted Sweet Potato and Black Bean Salad

MARKET ON MAIN, ROCKLAND

serves 6

2 pounds sweet potatoes, peeled and cut into 1-inch cubes
3 tablespoons olive oil
salt and freshly ground black pepper
3 cups cooked or canned black beans, rinsed and well drained
⅔ cup finely chopped red onion
1 red bell pepper, seeded and diced
1 green bell pepper, seeded and diced
¼ cup minced fresh cilantro
¼ cup chopped scallions
1–1 ½ cups Jalapeño-Lime Dressing (see below)

1. Preheat the oven to 375°F. Toss the cubed sweet potatoes with the olive oil, season with salt and pepper, and spread in a single layer on a baking sheet. Roast, stirring occasionally, until the potatoes are tender and brown, about 25 minutes. Set aside to cool.
2. To assemble the salad, combine the roasted potatoes with the beans and all the remaining ingredients. Add 1 cup of the dressing and toss. Add additional dressing and salt and pepper to taste.

Jalapeño-Lime Dressing

MARKET ON MAIN, ROCKLAND

makes 1 ½ cups

⅓ cup fresh-squeezed lime juice
2 tablespoons balsamic vinegar
1 tablespoon prepared Dijon mustard
1 teaspoon chopped fresh garlic
1 jalapeño pepper, seeded and chopped
¼ teaspoon salt
1 cup olive oil

In a blender or food processor, combine the lime juice, vinegar, mustard, garlic, jalapeño, and salt. With the motor running, slowly drizzle in the olive oil to make a thick emulsion.

Black Bean, Barley, and Fresh Corn Salad

CHERIE'S, KENNEBUNK

serves 8–10

2 cups water
1 cup barley
1 ½ cups corn kernels, cut fresh from the cob or frozen
1 cup diced, seeded fresh tomatoes
⅓ cup finely chopped cilantro leaves
1 red bell pepper, seeded and diced
¼ cup chopped scallions
½ cup finely chopped red onion
3 cups cooked black beans, well drained
¼ cup fresh lemon juice
1 tablespoon olive oil
1 teaspoon jalapeño hot pepper sauce, or more to taste
½ teaspoon ground cumin
½ teaspoon salt
½ teaspoon black pepper

1. Bring the water to a boil in a saucepan. Stir in the barley, cover, and simmer for about 30 minutes, or until the barley is tender. Rinse the barley under cold running water and drain well.
2. In a salad bowl, toss the barley with all the remaining ingredients. Cover and chill before serving.

Julie's Salad of Fruits and Greens with Pumpkin Seed Oil Vinaigrette

CAFÉ THIS WAY, BAR HARBOR

serves 6 as a first course

Chef Julie Harris at Café This Way created this salad to show off her delicious Austrian pumpkin seed oil, a gift from a friend who brought it all the way from Europe. When the oil ran out, Julie had to search for a replacement and found it— where else?—on the Internet.

You've got no pumpkin seed oil on hand? Try another fragrant nut oil in its place, such as hazelnut or walnut oil, or just go with a trusty extra-virgin olive oil.

For the vinaigrette:

2 cloves garlic
½ cup orange juice (fresh-squeezed is best)
½ cup red wine vinegar
¼ cup soy sauce
½ cup pumpkin seed oil
½ cup vegetable oil

In a food processor, purée the garlic with the orange juice, vinegar, and soy sauce. With the motor running, slowly drizzle in the pumpkin seed oil, then the vegetable oil, to make a thick, emulsified dressing.

For the salad:

1 pound garden greens or store-bought mixed salad greens such as mesclun, arugula, baby spinach, leaf lettuce, or any combination
1 cup seedless grapes (red or white)
1 Granny Smith apple, unpeeled
1 ripe pear, unpeeled
8 ounces crumbled fresh goat cheese
⅓ cup coarsely chopped walnuts or pecans

1. Wash, dry, and chill the greens before assembling the salad.
2. Just before serving, quarter, core, and thinly slice the apple and the pear. (Do this at the very last minute—the fruit will darken if you slice it ahead of time.)
3. Add all the fruit to the greens in a big salad bowl and toss with vinaigrette to taste. Top with the crumbled goat cheese and nuts and serve.

Garlicky Tabouli

LOMPOC CAFÉ, BAR HARBOR

serves 8–10

1 ½ cups dry bulgur
2 ¼ cups boiling water
4 plum tomatoes, seeded and diced
1 medium red onion, diced (about ⅔ cup)
⅓ cup minced fresh parsley
¼ cup minced fresh mint
1 tablespoon finely minced fresh garlic
2 tablespoons olive oil
¼ teaspoon salt
½ teaspoon freshly ground black pepper
½ cup fresh-squeezed lemon juice
1 cup crumbled feta cheese (optional)
½ cup pitted black olives (optional)

1. Place the bulgur in a large bowl and pour the boiling water over it. Cover and let stand for at least 3 hours, until the water is absorbed and the bulgur has a soft but chewy texture.
2. Add the remaining ingredients—except the feta cheese and olives—and toss well.
3. Season to taste with more salt and pepper if needed. Serve immediately topped with the feta and olives.

Note: If you chill leftover tabouli, the wheat may absorb all the olive oil. To moisten the tabouli, just add an additional tablespoon of oil, toss, and serve.

Hummus Goes to Italy

CAFÉ MIRANDA, ROCKLAND

serves 6 as an appetizer

Hummus can do more than you think. We know it as a spread that goes on anything—crusty breads, crackers, bagels, and pita rounds—but at Café Miranda, Kerry Altiero converts a batch of hummus into a sauce for a colorful chilled pasta dish with the addition of some diced ripe tomatoes.

The beauty of hummus, says Kerry, is that it needs "zero cooking!"

1 can (14–16 ounces) garbanzo beans (also called ceci beans or chickpeas)
1 can (14–16 ounces) artichoke hearts packed in water
½ cup extra-virgin olive oil, plus a bit more to drizzle on top
3 cloves fresh garlic, chopped, or more to taste
¼ cup water
salt and freshly ground black pepper to taste
½ cup finely chopped flat-leaf parsley, plus 2 tablespoons for garnish
1 lemon, cut into thick wedges

1. Rinse and thoroughly drain the beans and the artichoke hearts, keeping them separate. Coarsely chop the artichoke hearts and set them aside in a mixing bowl.
2. Toss the beans with the olive oil, garlic, and water. Season with a bit of salt and pepper. In a blender or food processor, purée the mixture in batches until it's smooth and creamy, adding the hummus to the bowl with the chopped artichokes as you go.
3. Fold in the ½ cup of parsley and season the mixture to taste with additional salt and pepper if needed.
4. To serve as an appetizer, spread the hummus on salad plates, drizzle with olive oil, sprinkle on the remaining parsley, and serve with lemon wedges, bread, pita, or crackers.

Evan and Kerry Altiero tend Miranda's brick oven.

Cool Hummus and Artichoke Pasta

COURTESY THE AUTHOR

serves 4

> 1 pound string pasta (linguine or spaghetti)
> 1 batch Hummus Goes to Italy (see p. 77), plus ¼–½ cup water (see Note)
> 2 ripe tomatoes, seeded and diced

1. Cook the pasta al dente, drain, and rinse thoroughly under cold running water.
2. In a big pasta or salad bowl, toss the hummus mixture with the pasta.
3. Serve the pasta (cool or at room temperature) on individual plates, topped with chopped tomatoes, additional olive oil, and parsley. Don't forget the lemon wedges.

Note: You can add the water to the hummus as you purée the bean mixture, or gently stir it in after the artichokes have been added.

Tuna Fish Salad Niçoise

MARKET ON MAIN, ROCKLAND

enough for 4 big sandwiches

This tuna fish salad can be piled on thick slices of sourdough, along with lettuce and tomato slices, or served over a salad of mixed greens. Toss this batch with 2 cups of chilled, cooked pasta, such as penne, fusilli, or cavatappi, to make a tuna-pasta salad.

> 3 cans (6 ounces each) chunk white tuna, well drained
> ⅔ cup mayonnaise
> 2 tablespoons olive oil
> 1 teaspoon minced fresh garlic
> 2 teaspoons prepared Dijon mustard
> ½ cup sliced pitted kalamata olives, or any type of pitted olive
> 1 tablespoon capers
> ½ cup chopped roasted red pepper
> 2 tablespoons minced red onion
> 2 tablespoons minced flat-leaf parsley

Flake the tuna in a mixing bowl. In a separate bowl, whisk together the mayonnaise, olive oil, garlic, and mustard until smooth. Add the dressing and all the remaining ingredients to the tuna and toss to combine.

Lemon Cashew Couscous Salad

LOMPOC CAFÉ, BAR HARBOR

serves 6

This couscous salad has the distinctive Asian flavor of toasted sesame seed oil paired with fresh lemon. Serve this with grilled chicken or fish.

    5 cups prepared couscous, at room temperature
    3 tablespoons olive oil
    2 tablespoons toasted sesame seed oil
    3 tablespoons freshly squeezed lemon juice
    ¼ cup chopped scallions
    ¼ cup diced red bell pepper
    ¼ cup grated or shredded carrots
    ¼ cup currants, soaked in 1 cup hot water for 10 minutes, then drained
    ¾ cup roasted unsalted cashews, coarsely chopped (or whole if you prefer)
    1 teaspoon minced fresh garlic
    2 tablespoons minced fresh parsley
    salt and freshly ground black pepper to taste

Combine all the ingredients in a large bowl and toss. Season to taste and serve immediately. If you refrigerate the salad, the couscous may absorb the liquids. To moisten it, just add 1 tablespoon each olive oil and lemon juice and toss before serving.

Italian Pasta Salad

LOMPOC CAFÉ, BAR HARBOR

serves 8

Here's an easy-to-assemble vinaigrette pasta salad, with a menu of additions to play with. This recipe can be doubled to make a great big batch.

5 cups (about 1 ½ pounds) dried pasta—a sturdy, bite-sized type such as rotini, fusilli, radiatore, or cavatappi
½ cup olive oil
¼ cup sliced pitted kalamata olives
¼ cup chopped fresh basil, or 1 tablespoon dried
1 tablespoon finely minced garlic
1 cup diced red bell pepper
1 tablespoon fresh-squeezed lemon juice
2 tablespoons red wine vinegar
3 tablespoon balsamic vinegar
salt and freshly ground black pepper to taste

1. Cook the pasta al dente in a large pot of boiling water. Drain and rinse immediately in very cold running water. Shake the pasta as dry as possible.
2. Place all the remaining ingredients in a large bowl and stir to combine. Add the pasta and toss well. Season to taste. Cover and let rest at room temperature for at least half an hour before serving. (If you must hold the pasta salad in the refrigerator before it is served, you may need to add additional olive oil and lemon juice to moisten it.)

Italian Pasta Salad Variations

To make a heartier salad, perfect for a summer dinner, add any of the following:
- Diced ripe tomatoes, or cherry tomatoes
- Chopped sun-dried tomatoes
- Diced precooked meats—chicken, tuna, smoked turkey, or ham
- Diced pepperoni or salami
- Chopped artichoke hearts
- Marinated mushrooms
- Chunks of fresh or regular mozzarella, Brie, feta, or Cheddar cheese
- Grated Asiago, Parmesan, or Romano cheese

Creative Coastal Cooking

Chapter 4

Breakfast, Brunch, and Fresh-Baked

Eggs, Hash, Pancakes, and...Tacos? —Plus Breads, Buns, and Muffins

At Local 188

Hollandaise Sauce for Eggs Benedict

THOMASTON CAFÉ, THOMASTON

sauce for 6–8 poached eggs

Use this classic on eggs Benedict or steamed vegetables.

"Our eggs Benedict are out of the ordinary because of our hollandaise sauce. We use thinly sliced Virginia ham instead of the usual thick slice of Canadian bacon, and sometimes we layer on ripe sliced tomatoes, lobster meat, avocado, or whatever looks good that day. But the hollandaise sauce is always the same—thick, rich, and quite puckery, with a fresh batch made every two hours."

—HERBERT PETERS, CHEF-OWNER, THOMASTON CAFÉ

6 egg yolks from very fresh large eggs
2 tablespoons cider vinegar
1 tablespoon fresh-squeezed lemon juice
½ teaspoon salt
¼ teaspoon ground white pepper
2 shakes Tabasco
¾ cup (1 ½ sticks) unsalted butter, melted

1. In a heavy, stainless-steel mixing bowl (or in the top of a double boiler), whisk together the egg yolks, vinegar, lemon juice, salt, pepper, and Tabasco.
2. Place the bowl over a pot of simmering water, but do not let the bottom of the bowl come into contact with the water. Continue to whisk until the mixture begins to thicken, or coat the back of a wooden spoon.
3. Once the mixture is thickened and hot, place it on a damp towel or other work surface and add the melted butter little by little as you whisk. Assemble the eggs Benedict according to your taste, and spoon on the hollandaise.

Herbert Peters & friends at Thomaston Café

Breakfast Fish Cakes

THOMASTON CAFÉ, THOMASTON

makes 8 cakes

The traditional fish cakes at Thomaston Café have a delicate texture and rich flavor. They make a delicious main course for lunch or dinner but, for a real coastal breakfast, top them with poached eggs and Herbert Peters's lemony hollandaise sauce (see p. 82).

¼ cup (½ stick) unsalted butter
1 cup minced onion
½ cup minced celery
½ cup heavy cream
1 pound halibut, haddock, or other firm white fish fillet, all skin and
   bones removed
2 ½ cups coarse fresh bread crumbs
2 large eggs, lightly beaten
1 tablespoon prepared Dijon mustard
1 tablespoon snipped fresh dill (or 1 ½ teaspoons dried)
1 tablespoon fresh-squeezed lemon juice
1 teaspoon freshly grated lemon zest
½ teaspoon kosher salt, or to taste
¼ teaspoon freshly ground white pepper
vegetable oil, for cooking fish cakes (about ½ cup)
lemon wedges

1. Melt the butter in a large, heavy skillet. Add the onion and celery, cover, and cook over medium-low heat, stirring occasionally, until the vegetables are soft. Don't let the mixture brown.
2. Add the cream and fish and simmer, covered, until the fish is just cooked through (about 5 to 7 minutes). Remove the skillet from the heat and cool the mixture slightly. Use a fork to break up and flake the fish, leaving plenty of meaty bits. Transfer the mixture to a large bowl.
3. Add the bread crumbs and all remaining ingredients—except the vegetable oil and lemon wedges. Toss the mixture to blend. Cover and chill for at least 1 hour, or overnight.
4. Using a ½-cup measure, scoop out the mixture to form patties, then place the cakes on a baking sheet lined with waxed paper.
5. Brush a griddle or well-seasoned cast-iron skillet with the oil and place over medium-high heat until it's hot, but not smoking. Cook the fish cakes in batches, about 2 minutes per side, or until golden. Serve with lemon wedges.

Café This Way
Corned Beef Hash

CAFÉ THIS WAY, BAR HARBOR

serves 6

Café This Way is a favorite breakfast spot in Bar Harbor, with locals and tourists willing to line up for a table while nursing a hot mug of coffee. Pounds and pounds of this hash are served every day, topped with poached or fried eggs.

1 pound redskin potatoes, unpeeled
1 pound cooked corned beef, diced
½ cup diced white onion
3 tablespoons Worcestershire sauce
hot sauce to taste
3–4 tablespoons vegetable or canola oil
salt and freshly ground black pepper to taste

1. Boil the potatoes in their skins until tender. Drain and set aside to cool completely.
2. Dice the potatoes and, in a large bowl, toss together with the corned beef, onion, Worcestershire sauce, and hot sauce.
3. In a large skillet, heat 3 tablespoons of the oil. Add the hash and sauté over medium-high heat until brown and crispy, adding more oil as needed. Season to taste with salt and pepper.

Creative Coastal Cooking

Wild Mushroom Breakfast Hash

THOMASTON CAFÉ, THOMASTON

serves 4

This hash is popular with vegetarians, who love to do brunch at the café. The portobellos give this hash a meaty flavor, so it's great topped with poached eggs and hollandaise sauce (see Index) or as a side dish with eggs any way you like them.

2 tablespoons olive oil
½ cup diced onion
½ cup diced red pepper
2 cloves garlic, minced
1 pound mixed mushrooms, including wild mushrooms if available, and white or cremini mushrooms
1 pound portobello mushrooms with their stems, sliced
3 cups peeled, diced potatoes
1 cup vegetable stock (see Index)
½ teaspoon salt and freshly ground black pepper to taste
vegetable oil, for frying

1. Heat the oil in a large skillet. Add the onion, red pepper, and garlic and sauté for about 5 minutes. Add all the mushrooms and cook for 10 minutes more as they release their juices.
2. Add the diced potatoes and the stock and simmer until the potatoes are tender. Season to taste. Set the hash aside to cool for at least 30 minutes, or until cool enough to handle.
3. Heat about 2 tablespoons of vegetable oil on a griddle or in a frying pan. Shape the hash into 4 large, omelet-sized patties. Fry them, turning once, until crisp and browned on both sides.

Sunday Brunch, Thomaston Café.

Chicken-Potato Hash Pancakes

THOMASTON CAFÉ, THOMASTON

makes 8 patties

Walk in the door of Thomaston Café on any Sunday morning and you'll smell baked goods fresh out of the oven, and bacon on the grill. Herbert Peters's menu features some real originals, not just standard breakfast fare—eggs on fish cakes or chicken hash fritters, for instance. He uses "leftovers" to assemble this dish, but to make these "pancakes," it's worth starting from scratch.

2 cups leftover cooked chicken meat, skinless, boneless
2 cups leftover home fries
1 medium onion, finely diced
broth or water as needed
¼ cup (½ stick) butter

1. Place the chicken, home fries, and onion in a food processor and pulse to a coarse consistency, adding a tablespoon or two of chicken broth or water to wet the mixture so that it holds together enough to form patties.
2. Make 8 oval patties. Melt the butter in a frying pan and sauté until brown and crisp on both sides. Serve topped with a soft poached or fried egg and hollandaise sauce, if you like.

In the kitchen, Thomaston Café

Ham and Potato Pancakes with Roasted Garlic Sour Cream

CHERIE'S, KENNEBUNK

serves 6

These savory pancakes can be served alone, or with eggs on the side. The Roasted Garlic Sour Cream can be used on baked or roasted potatoes, too.

For the Ham and Potato Cakes:

2 large russet potatoes, peeled and grated
4 ounces cooked ham, diced
1 tablespoon chopped parsley
1 tablespoon chopped scallions
2 eggs, beaten
2 tablespoons flour
¼ teaspoon salt
¼ teaspoon pepper
¼ cup olive oil, for frying

1. Drain the potatoes thoroughly in a colander to shake out any excess liquid, or pat dry between layers of paper towels.
2. In a mixing bowl, combine the potatoes, ham, parsley, scallions, and eggs. Sprinkle the flour over the mixture and blend well. Season with salt and pepper.
3. Heat 2 tablespoon of the olive oil in a heavy skillet. When the skillet is hot, ladle in 3 pancakes, using half the batter. Fry until golden brown, about 4 minutes per side. Repeat with the remaining oil and batter. Serve topped with Roasted Garlic Sour Cream.

For the Roasted Garlic Sour Cream:

1 cup sour cream
1 tablespoon puréed roasted garlic (see Index)
1 teaspoon minced fresh parsley
a pinch of salt

Whisk all the ingredients until smooth. Cover and chill until ready to use.

Dave's Tortilla de Patatas

LOCAL 188, PORTLAND

serves 8–10

The crowd at Local 188 consumes tons of this stuff. In keeping with the restaurant's homage to Spanish cuisine, this is chef Dave Noyes's version of tortilla de patatas, a staple of Spanish cooking. It's a big, oven-baked omelet, loaded with potatoes, peppers, and onions. This is a great dish for a brunch buffet—it's delicious warm, or at room temperature—but in Spain (and Portland) it's eaten at any time of day.

    10 tablespoons olive oil
    3 cups chopped Spanish onion
    4 red bell peppers, seeded and diced
    ¼ cup dry white wine
    5 large Yukon Gold potatoes (about 3 pounds), peeled and coarsely chopped
    1 teaspoon smoky or hot paprika
    1 ½ teaspoons salt
    ½ teaspoon fresh black pepper
    20 eggs, beaten
    4 ounces goat cheese
    3 chopped scallions

1. Preheat the oven to 350°F.
2. Heat 2 tablespoons of the olive oil in a large skillet. Add the onion and bell peppers and sauté over high heat until the onion begins to brown. Deglaze the pan with the wine.

David Noyes, Local 188

3. In a shallow roasting pan, toss the potatoes with 4 tablespoons of the olive oil, the paprika, salt, and pepper. Bake for 20 minutes, stirring twice to coat the potatoes with oil.
4. When the potatoes are done, heat the remaining 4 tablespoons of olive oil in a large cast-iron casserole or Dutch oven. Pour in a third of the beaten eggs, stirring as they cook in the hot oil. In layers, add half the roasted potatoes, all the sautéed onion and peppers, then the remaining potatoes. Press down lightly on the top, then pour in the rest of the beaten eggs.
5. Crumble the goat cheese over the eggs and top with the chopped scallions. Bake for 50 to 60 minutes, or until set.

Breakfast Tacos with Chorizo and Tomato-Avocado Salsa

CHERIE'S, KENNEBUNK

serves 4

If you don't have chorizo on hand, improvise by using regular bulk sausage spiced up with ½ teaspoon each of ground cumin and chili powder, and a pinch of cayenne pepper.

For the Tomato-Avocado Salsa:

6 ripe plum tomatoes, seeded and diced
½ cup finely diced red onion
2 teaspoons minced fresh garlic
fresh juice of 2 limes
1 tablespoon rice wine vinegar
1 ripe avocado, peeled and diced

In a bowl, combine all the ingredients—except the avocado—and season to taste with salt and pepper. Gently fold in the avocado.

For the tacos:

2 tablespoons butter
8 ounces chorizo sausage, removed from casings
6 eggs, beaten
4 crisp taco shells
½ cup grated Pepper Jack cheese
½ cup sour cream

1. Melt the butter in a skillet. Add the chorizo and cook until brown. Add the eggs and scramble them with the sausage.
2. Quickly assemble the tacos while the eggs are hot: Divide the sausage and eggs among the taco shells, then top each with 2 tablespoons of grated cheese, followed by a spoonful of salsa and a dollop of sour cream. Serve immediately.

Jack French Toast

serves 6–8

Or you can call it Jack's French toast—it's named after Jack French, a Rogue River friend and regular.

1 tablespoon soft butter
4 eggs
1 cup whole milk
1 cup heavy cream
6 tablespoons sugar
1 ½ teaspoons cinnamon
a pinch of salt
1 teaspoon vanilla extract
half a large loaf of good-quality bread, such as brioche, challah, or homemade
    white bread
½ cup golden raisins
additional butter, for frying
maple syrup
powdered sugar, for dusting

1. Preheat the oven to 325°F. Use the butter to coat a 9 x 13-inch glass baking dish.
2. Beat the eggs until light, then whisk in the milk, cream, sugar, cinnamon, salt, and vanilla.
3. Cut the bread into ½-inch-thick slices, with crusts trimmed. Loosely fit a single layer of slices into the bottom of the baking dish. Pour one-third of the cream mixture over the bread, then sprinkle with half the raisins. Follow with another layer of bread, one-third of the cream mixture, and the remaining raisins. Finish with a final layer of bread and the remaining cream mixture.
4. Cover the dish first with a sheet of parchment paper, then cover tightly with foil. Bake for 1 hour. Remove the pan from the oven and cool. Refrigerate if not using immediately.
5. To serve, heat 2 tablespoons of butter in a skillet. Cut the French toast into squares and sauté in the butter until hot and golden brown, using additional butter as needed. Serve with hot maple syrup and dusted with powdered sugar.

Crispy Banana-Stuffed French Toast

CHERIE'S, KENNEBUNK

serves 2

Chefs love panko Japanese-style bread crumbs. They're made from rice flour and, when used to coat fried foods, result in a light but very crispy crust. They are often found in specialty grocery stores but, if you can't find them, ask a local chef. In any case, this dish can be made with or without the bread crumb coating.

2 ripe bananas
½ teaspoon ground nutmeg
1 teaspoon cinnamon
2 teaspoons sugar
4 slices good white bread
3 eggs, beaten
1 cup whole milk or cream
2 cups panko bread crumbs
¼ cup (½ stick) butter

1. Mash the bananas with the nutmeg, cinnamon, and sugar.
2. Spread the banana mixture generously over the bread slices, then make 2 sandwiches.
3. Beat the eggs and milk (or cream) together in a wide bowl or pie plate and place the panko bread crumbs in a similar dish.
4. Melt the butter in a large, nonstick skillet over medium heat.
5. Dip each "sandwich" in the egg mixture, turning and coating completely, then dip in the bread crumbs, coating both sides again. Place immediately in the hot skillet and fry until golden brown, about 4 or 5 minutes per side. Serve with warm maple syrup.

Basic Scones

MORNING GLORY BAKERY, BAR HARBOR

makes 8 big scones

3 cups flour
4 teaspoons baking powder
a scant pinch of salt
¾ cup (1 ½ sticks) chilled butter, cut into pieces
3 eggs
¼ cup whole milk
2 tablespoons honey
¼ cup melted butter

1. Preheat the oven to 375°F. Line a baking sheet with waxed or parchment paper.
2. In the bowl of a standing electric mixer fitted with a dough hook attachment, combine the flour, baking powder, and salt. Add the butter and blend into the dry ingredients. If mixing by hand, use a pastry blender, or a large-tined fork, to cut the butter into the dry ingredients to make a coarse meal.

   Note: If you are making scones with added ingredients from the list below, fold them in now.

3. In a separate mixing bowl, whisk together the eggs, milk, and honey. Add to the dough and stir until just blended.
4. Turn the batter onto a lightly floured work surface, knead once or twice dusting with flour, and form the dough into a round, flat disc 1 ½ inches thick. Use a rolling pin lightly if needed.
5. Cut the disc into 8 uniform wedges and transfer to the lined baking sheet.
6. Brush the scones generously with the melted butter and bake until light golden brown, about 20 minutes.

Fancy Scones

Use the basic recipe to make plain scones, or add creative ingredient combinations to make fancier versions. For some favorites of Ralph McDonnell and Anna Durand, owners of Morning Glory Bakery, add:

- ⅓ cup chopped hazelnuts, plus ⅓ cup white chocolate chips
- ⅓ cup chopped walnuts, ⅓ cup dried cranberries, plus 1 teaspoon grated fresh orange zest
- ⅓ cup chopped dates, ⅓ cup chopped pecans, plus 1 teaspoon cinnamon
- ⅓ cup dried cherries, ⅓ cup chopped almonds, plus ½ teaspoon ground cloves

Sour Cream Streusel Coffee

one 10-inch bundt cake

For the streusel mixture:

¼ cup (½ stick) soft butter
3 tablespoons granulated sugar
2 tablespoons brown sugar
¾ cup flour
1 teaspoon cinnamon
¼ cup rolled oats
½ cup walnut pieces
a scant pinch of salt

For the coffee cake:

¾ cup (1 ½ sticks) butter
1 cup sugar
3 teaspoons vanilla extract
4 eggs
2 ⅔ cups flour
1 ½ teaspoons baking powder
1 ¼ teaspoons baking soda
½ teaspoon salt
1 ⅓ cups sour cream

1. Generously butter a 10-inch bundt pan. Preheat the oven to 375°F.
2. To make the streusel topping, place all the ingredients in the bowl of a food processor and pulse a few times to make a coarse, crumbly mixture. If mixing by hand, toss the ingredients together with a spatula in a small mixing bowl. Reserve.
3. Using an electric mixer, cream together the butter, sugar, and vanilla until light and fluffy. Beat in the eggs one at a time.
4. Sift together the dry ingredients, then add to the butter-and-egg mixture by thirds, alternating with the sour cream. Do not beat the batter; mix just until blended.
5. Spread half the batter into the bundt pan. Top evenly with half the streusel mixture. Carefully spread the remaining batter over the streusel and top with the remaining streusel mixture.
6. Bake for 50 to 60 minutes, or until a tester inserted in the cake comes out clean.
7. Cool the cake in the pan on a cooling rack. Loosen the rim of the cake with a knife before turning it out onto a cake plate.

Vegan Morning Glory Muffins

MORNING GLORY BAKERY, BAR HARBOR

makes a big batch—2 dozen muffins or more

"You can make this batter and leave it in the fridge for a week, scooping and baking the muffins as you need them. The true vegan may want to substitute corn syrup for the honey."

—RALPH MCDONNELL, OWNER, MORNING GLORY BAKERY

1 ¼ cups boiling water
3 ½ cups bran
3 ¼ cups flour (white, whole wheat, or a combination)
4 teaspoons baking powder
4 teaspoons baking soda
1 tablespoon salt
2 tablespoons cinnamon
1 ½ cups grated peeled carrots
1 cup chopped pecans
1 cup shredded unsweetened coconut
1 cup raisins
2 tablespoons fresh-squeezed lemon juice
2 ½ cups soy milk
½ cup canola or safflower oil
1 cup honey

1. Pour the boiling water over the bran, cover, and let rest for 1 hour.
2. In a large mixing bowl, toss together the flour, baking powder, baking soda, salt, and cinnamon until blended. Add the carrots, pecans, coconut, and raisins and toss to coat with the dry ingredients.
3. In a small mixing bowl, whisk together the lemon juice, soy milk, oil, and honey. Pour the mixture into the dry ingredients and stir with a wide spatula until the batter is just blended. Cover and refrigerate until ready to use.
4. To bake the muffins, preheat the oven to 375°F, grease a muffin pan, and line it with paper muffin cups. Fill the cups two-thirds full with batter and bake for 20 to 25 minutes, or until a tester inserted in the center of a muffin comes out clean.

Wild Blueberry Muffins

MORNING GLORY BAKERY, BAR HARBOR

makes 12 big muffins

To make light, fluffy muffins, avoid overmixing the batter.

1 cup plus 2 tablespoons butter, softened
1 cup plus 2 tablespoons sugar
3 eggs
1 ½ teaspoons vanilla extract
3 ¼ cups flour
1 tablespoon baking powder
1 ½ teaspoons salt
1 ½ cups whole milk
2 cup fresh blueberries (or substitute frozen berries)

1. Preheat the oven to 375°F. Grease a 12-cup muffin tin.
2. Using an electric mixer, or by hand, beat together the butter and sugar until light and fluffy. Beat in the eggs one at a time. Add the vanilla.
3. In a large mixing bowl, toss together the flour, baking powder, and salt. Add half the milk and stir until just barely mixed. Fold in the butter-and-egg mixture with a few turns of a spatula.
4. Add the remaining milk and the fruit and stir minimally, just three or four strokes, to make a lumpy batter.
5. Scoop the batter into the muffin tin and bake about 20 to 25 minutes, or until a tester inserted in the center of a muffin comes out clean. Let the muffins cool completely in the pan before attempting to remove them.

Frosted English Currant Buns

PRIMO, ROCKLAND

makes 2 dozen

"The frosting turns these delicious buns into a special treat. They're great for breakfast, but are especially well suited for afternoon tea."

—MELISSA KELLY, CHEF-OWNER, PRIMO

For the currant buns:

½ cup dried currants
1 cup water
½ cup butter
1 teaspoon sugar
¼ teaspoon salt
1 cup flour
4 eggs

1. Preheat the oven to 375°F. Have ready a generously greased baking sheet.
2. Place the currants in a bowl and add about 2 cups boiling water to plump. Set aside.
3. In a large saucepan, combine the 1 cup of water, butter, sugar, and salt. Bring to a boil. Add the flour all at once, lower the heat, and beat until the mixture leaves the sides of the pan. Remove from the heat and stir until slightly cooled.
4. Add the eggs, one at a time, beating well after each addition. Drain the currants and add them to the batter, stirring well.
5. Drop the batter by rounded tablespoons, about 1 inch apart, onto the baking sheet. Bake for 30 minutes, until light golden brown. Remove from the oven and cool on a rack.

For the frosting:

1 tablespoon butter
1 ½ tablespoons heavy cream
¾ cup powdered sugar
1 teaspoon vanilla extract

1. Melt the butter in a small pan. Stir in the cream and remove from the heat.
2. Stir in the powdered sugar and vanilla and beat well. Chill for 1 hour.
3. When the buns are completely cool, top each generously with frosting.

Big Swedish Cardamom Buns

MORNING GLORY BAKERY, BAR HARBOR

makes 2 dozen

3 ½ tablespoons dry yeast
¾ cup sugar
1 ½ teaspoons salt
2 cups warm milk
1 pound (4 sticks) butter, at room temperature
9 cups unbleached white flour
1 tablespoon ground cardamom
3 eggs
1 cup raisins
1 whole egg beaten with 2 tablespoons milk, for the egg wash

1. To make the buns in a standing electric mixer, put the yeast, sugar, salt, and warm milk in the mixer bowl and beat, using the dough hook attachment set on medium speed. Incorporate the butter by large spoonfuls, then slowly add the flour and cardamom.
2. Add the eggs one at a time, then the raisins.
3. Shift to low speed to knead the dough until very smooth, about 7 minutes.

   Note: If you are making the buns by hand, combine the ingredients with a spatula in a large bowl as directed above, then turn out the dough onto a flour-dusted work surface and knead for 7 to 10 minutes.

4. Place the dough in a lightly oiled bowl, cover with a kitchen towel, and let rise until double in bulk.
5. To form the buns, punch down the dough and divide in half, then into quarters. Pull 4 buns from each quarter, rolling them against a flour-dusted work surface to form round balls (about 6 ounces each). Place the balls on a lightly oiled baking sheet and allow to rise again—in a warm, draftless area—until double in bulk.
6. Preheat the oven to 350°F. Brush the buns with the egg wash and bake until golden brown, about 12 to 15 minutes. The buns are done when they sound hollow when tapped on the bottom.

Focaccia—Herbed Italian Flatbread—and Variations

Morning Glory Bakery, Bar Harbor

Basic Focaccia

make 2 loaves

2 ½–3 cups flour
1 ¼ cups water
1 tablespoon dry active yeast
½ cup extra-virgin olive oil, plus additional for baking
2 teaspoons regular salt
2 teaspoons mixed dried herbs (rosemary, thyme, oregano)
kosher or sea salt to taste

1. Starting with 2 ½ cups flour, put the water, yeast, ½ cup olive oil, and regular salt in the bowl of a standing electric mixer. Using the dough hook attachment set on medium speed, blend until smooth. To mix by hand, place the ingredients in a large mixing bowl and blend with a wide spatula.
2. Add the additional ½ cup flour, if needed, to make a dough sticky enough to gather into a ball. Place the dough in an oiled bowl, cover with a kitchen towel, and let rise in a warm place until double in bulk.
3. Punch down the dough and turn it out onto a lightly floured work surface. Divide the dough in half and roll into two ½-inch-thick rounds, or rectangles, if you prefer. Place the dough on a lightly greased baking sheet and let rise again until it is 1 inch thick.
4. Preheat the oven to 350°F. Before baking the focaccia, lightly poke the surface all over with your fingertips to make indentations. Brush with olive oil and sprinkle on the dried herbs and kosher or sea salt to taste.
5. Bake the flatbread until light golden, about 20 minutes. Brush with additional olive oil as soon as the loaves come out of the oven. Serve warm.

Curried Potato Stuffed Focaccia

makes 4 small loaves

1 batch Basic Focaccia dough (see above)
¼ cup olive oil
¼ cup finely chopped onion
1 teaspoon minced garlic
3 cups peeled, coarsely chopped cooked potatoes

1 teaspoon ground coriander
1 teaspoon ground cumin
¼ teaspoon cinnamon
¼ teaspoon cayenne
2 teaspoons curry powder
1 teaspoon paprika
¼ teaspoon black pepper
1 teaspoon salt

1. Prepare the Basic Focaccia dough. Roll the dough out in a ¾-inch-thick rectangle and place on a lightly greased baking sheet.
2. Heat the olive oil in a large skillet. Add the onion and garlic and sauté for 5 minutes. Add the potatoes, and all the remaining ingredients, and sauté until well blended, mashing the potatoes a bit as you go. Set aside to cool for 20 minutes.
3. Spread the cooled potato mixture evenly over the focaccia, then roll the dough like a jelly roll, and crimp the seam. Slice the roll into 4 equal pieces. Let rise until doubled in bulk.
4. Preheat the oven to 350°F. Brush the stuffed focaccia with olive oil and bake until light golden, about 20 minutes.

Ham and Havarti Stuffed Focaccia

makes 4 small loaves

1 batch Basic Focaccia dough (see p. 98)
2 tablespoons olive oil
½ cup finely chopped onion
½ cup chopped red bell pepper
1 cup diced cooked ham
2 teaspoons dried dill weed
¼ teaspoon freshly ground black pepper
½ cup grated Havarti cheese

1. Prepare the Basic Focaccia dough. Roll the dough out into a ¾-inch-thick rectangle and place on a lightly greased baking sheet.
2. Heat the olive oil in a skillet. Add the onion and bell pepper and sauté for 5 minutes. Add the ham, dill weed, and black pepper and sauté until the ham is lightly browned. Set aside to cool for 20 minutes.
3. Spread the cooled ham mixture evenly over the focaccia, sprinkle on the grated cheese, then roll the dough like a jelly roll and crimp the seam. Slice the roll into 4 equal pieces. Let rise until doubled in bulk.
4. Preheat the oven to 350°F. Brush the stuffed focaccia with olive oil and bake until light golden, about 20 minutes.

Daily Bread

THOMASTON CAFÉ, THOMASTON

"The many years of teaching young people the art of cooking have taught me quite a few lessons, a most vital one—to simplify. Here is a recipe that always works and is also fun to do."

—HERBERT PETERS, CHEF-OWNER, THOMASTON CAFÉ

In Herbert's words, this is the way to make a very traditional loaf of simple white bread, an exercise that satisfies the spirit as well as the appetite.

2 tablespoons (2 packages) active dry yeast
2 teaspoons granulated sugar
2 cups warm water
2 tablespoons vegetable or olive oil
2 teaspoons salt
4–5 cups all-purpose flour

"Combine the first 3 ingredients in a mixing bowl. Let sit till the yeast is coming to the surface of the water, about 2 minutes, then add the rest of the ingredients except for 1 cup of the flour. Mix with a wooden spoon or your hands.

"Put the dough on a floured table, using some of the remaining flour. Work (knead) the dough with your hands, about 200 turns or until the dough feels smooth and elastic, flouring your hands and the table as needed. Let the dough rest, covered with a kitchen towel. Depending on the temperature of the kitchen, the dough will take anywhere from 10 to 20 minutes to ferment. Test the dough by inserting your fingers into it, making holes. If the holes stay, the dough is ready for the next step. If the holes fill in, the dough needs more time.

"Next, punch the dough down to remove all the gases that have developed. Knead again for a minute. Then divide the dough in half. To make loaves of bread, roll one of the doughs into a long shape, the size of a cookie sheet, and taper the ends. Sprinkle the cookie sheet with cornmeal. Repeat with the rest of the dough.

"Now cover the loaves with a towel again and let rise for another 10 to 20 minutes. (Preheat the oven to 375°F.) Spray or brush the loaves with cold water. With a sharp knife, make a few ¼-inch-deep incisions over the top, cut on a slant. Put into the hot oven and bake for 25 to 30 minutes. The top should be browned and the loaves should feel hollow when tapped."

Creative Coastal Cooking

Porter Ale Bread

LOMPOC CAFÉ, BAR HARBOR

"This bread is so quick and easy to make, you won't believe how good it is. Of course, I make it with Lompoc's own Porter Ale, but any good-quality beer is just fine. It's best served while still warm out of the oven, with plenty of butter. If you have any left—and don't count on it—use it to make fantastic toast."

—CHEF LISE DESROCHERS

This "beer" bread is the perfect match for Lompoc Café's Burgundy Beef Stew (see Index). Cut a thick slice of the warm bread, place it in a wide soup bowl, and ladle the stew on top.

> 3 tablespoons melted butter
> 3 cups unbleached white flour
> 1 tablespoon baking powder
> 2 tablespoons plus 1 teaspoon sugar
> 1 teaspoon salt
> 1 ½ cups Porter Ale or other dark beer

1. Preheat the oven to 375°F. Brush a standard loaf pan with half the melted butter.
2. Place all the dry ingredients in a mixing bowl and toss with a spatula to combine.
3. Add the beer and mix quickly, folding the beer into the dry ingredients with just a few turns of the spatula. The dough should be lumpy, thick, and quite sticky.
4. Spoon the dough into the loaf pan and smooth the surface a little. Drizzle the remaining butter on top and bake for 45 to 50 minutes, until golden brown. Wait about 5 minutes, then turn the loaf out onto a cooling rack. Cool for about 10 minutes before slicing.

Chapter 5

Side Trips

SO MANY POTATOES, SO LITTLE TIME—PLUS
FRITTERS, DUMPLINGS, AND RICE

In Rockland Harbor

Making Mashed Potatoes

Skins-on, skins-off, lumpy or smooth, nobody doesn't like mashed potatoes, and that's why they've made a big comeback in contemporary restaurants.

Get creative with the Chunky Mashed Potatoes and Basic Mashed Russets recipes. You can add grated cheese, hot spice blends, bacon bits, herbs—anything that seems right with potatoes.

If you like home-style mashed potatoes with a slightly lumpy texture, use a handheld potato masher to achieve the desired consistency. If you prefer your mashed potatoes "whipped" and creamy, then push them through a potato ricer and beat them with an electric mixer as you add the cream.

MOM's Chunky Mashed Potatoes

MARKET ON MAIN, ROCKLAND

serves 4–6

4 medium Yukon Gold potatoes
1 medium sweet potato
2 cloves garlic
⅔ cup whole milk or cream
salt and freshly ground black pepper to taste
⅓ cup sour cream

1. Place all the potatoes (unpeeled) in a large pot. Cover with cold water; add the garlic cloves and 1 tablespoon of salt. Bring the pot to a boil, cover, and cook until the potatoes are fork-tender. Drain the potatoes and set them aside, along with the garlic cloves.
2. When the potatoes are cool enough to handle, pull or peel off the skins and trim away any eyes or dark spots.
3. Heat the milk in a large saucepan. Add the potatoes and garlic cloves and hand-mash to a chunky consistency. Season to taste with salt and pepper. Place the potatoes in a serving bowl and spoon the sour cream on top. Stir the sour cream into the top of the potatoes with a couple of turns of a spoon, leaving some swirls of sour cream visible on top.

Basic Mashed Russets

COURTESY THE AUTHOR

serves 8–10

For Roasted Garlic Mashed Potatoes: Beat in ⅓ cup puréed roasted garlic (see Index) along with the cream.

5 pounds fresh, firm russet (Idaho) potatoes
½ cup (1 stick) butter
1 cup finely minced white onion
1 teaspoon salt, or more to taste
1 cup heavy (whipping) cream

1. Peel the potatoes and quarter them lengthwise, dropping them into a large bowl of cold water as you go to prevent them from discoloring and to extract some of the starch.
2. Drain the potatoes and rinse them. Place them in a steamer basket in a large stockpot. Add enough water to reach the base of the steamer basket. Cover the pot and bring to a boil. Steam the potatoes just until they are fork-tender but still firm. Remove them from the pot and set them aside to cool in a colander.
3. Meanwhile, melt the butter over low heat in a heavy saucepan. Add the onion and cook for 15 to 20 minutes until soft and golden.
4. Place the dry stockpot over low heat. Add the potatoes and shake and toss them in the hot pot for a minute or two to steam off any excess water. Add the cooked onion and the salt.
5. Hand-mash for lumpy potatoes, or rice the potatoes and cooked onions together for a "whipped" texture. Beat in the cream and season with additional salt to taste.

Fancy Lobster Mashed Potatoes

THOMASTON CAFÉ, THOMASTON

serves 4

Very simple, but very fancy. Serve this as a very special side dish with grilled or baked fish—or pair it with a sizzling steak and you've got surf and turf.

½ cup (1 stick) unsalted butter
6 ounces lobster meat in coarse chunks
2 tablespoons brandy
¼ cup heavy cream
4 cups hot, prepared Basic Mashed Russets with Roasted Garlic (see above)
2 tablespoons snipped fresh chives

1. Melt the butter in a large skillet over medium-high heat. Toss in the lobster and sauté until it begins to brown.

2. Add the brandy, then tip the pan to one side and hold a match to the surface of the liquid. It should ignite, and the brandy should burn off in a minute or two. Needless to say, be careful—but it's really a simple technique. If you don't succeed in getting a nice blue flame, don't worry; just simmer until the brandy is reduced.
3. Remove half the sautéed lobster from the pan and set aside. Add the cream and the mashed potatoes to the skillet and fold together with the lobster and pan juices. When the mixture is hot, spoon it onto individual plates, or into a large serving bowl, and top with the reserved lobster. Garnish with the snipped chives.

Skins-On Garlic Mashed Yukon Golds

LOCAL 188, PORTLAND

serves 6–8

> 5 pounds Yukon Gold potatoes, well scrubbed
> 1 whole head of garlic, cloves separated but unpeeled
> ½ cup (1 stick) soft butter
> ½ cup whole milk or cream
> salt and Tabasco to taste

1. Trim any dark spots or eyes from the potatoes, then quarter them and place them in a large pot. Add water to cover the potatoes, along with 2 teaspoons of salt and the unpeeled garlic cloves.
2. Bring the pot to a boil and simmer, partially covered, for 15 to 20 minutes, or until the potatoes are fork-tender but not mushy.
3. In a colander, drain the potatoes thoroughly. Put the pot back on the rangetop and heat it over a low flame. When the pot is dry, add the cooked potatoes and shake or stir them until they are very dry and any excess water has evaporated. Squeeze the soft garlic from the skins and add to the potatoes.
4. Add the butter and milk (or cream) to the pot, along with 1 teaspoon of salt. Use a handheld potato masher to break up the potatoes to the desired consistency. Season with additional salt and Tabasco to taste.

Herb Roasted Potatoes

serves 6

Seeking out really freshly picked potatoes is well worth the effort. Like any vegetable, potatoes will lose some of their natural sweetness over time. Look for small organic varieties at farmer's markets. Add the optional coarse-grain mustard to this recipe for a little tartness, especially if you are serving the potatoes with roasted poultry.

3 pounds small, garden-fresh redskin or fingerling potatoes
¼ cup olive oil
2 teaspoons chopped fresh rosemary leaves
2 teaspoons chopped fresh thyme leaves
2 teaspoons minced fresh garlic, or more to taste
1 teaspoon salt
½ teaspoon freshly ground black pepper
2 tablespoons prepared coarse-grain mustard (optional)

1. Preheat the oven to 375°F. Thoroughly scrub and rinse the potatoes. Pat them dry and allow them to air-dry for about 1 hour before baking.
2. In a mixing bowl, whisk the olive oil with the herbs, garlic, salt, pepper, and mustard, if using. Add the potatoes and toss until coated.
3. Pour the potatoes into a baking dish or roasting pan large enough to hold them in a single layer. Bake for 40 to 50 minutes, or until browned and tender.

Brown Sugared Yams with Vanilla

PRIMO, ROCKLAND

serves 6–8

6 medium sweet potatoes, peeled and cut into large chunks
3 cups water
¾ cup granulated sugar
¾ cup light brown sugar
½ cup (1 stick) butter
1 tablespoon vanilla extract, or 1 fresh vanilla bean, split, with beans
    scraped into the pot
juice and zest from 1 lemon and 1 orange
2 cinnamon sticks
salt and freshly ground black pepper to taste

1. Preheat the oven to 350°F.
2. Place all the ingredients in a large pot and bring to a boil. Reduce the heat and simmer until the potatoes are just fork-tender, but still firm. Lift the potatoes from the pot with a slotted spoon and place them in a casserole dish.
3. Reduce the liquids by half and pour them over the potatoes. Bake for 15 to 20 minutes, until the potatoes are glazed and bubbly.

Melissa Kelly's Blue Cheese Potato Gratin

PRIMO, ROCKLAND

serves 6-8

This dish can be made in advance, then reheated.

8 large Yukon Gold potatoes, peeled and sliced ⅛ inch thick
2 cups heavy cream
1 cup crumbled Maytag blue cheese
salt and freshly ground black pepper to taste
2 teaspoons chopped fresh thyme leaves

1. Preheat the oven to 400°F. Set aside a casserole dish or deep cast-iron skillet.
2. Gently toss the sliced potatoes with all the other ingredients to coat.
3. Layer the mixture in the casserole or skillet. Cover with foil and bake for 45 minutes, or until the potatoes are fork-tender.
4. Remove the foil and continue to bake until golden brown, about 15 minutes more.

More Potato Gratin Variations

Classic Scalloped Potatoes and Onions

serves 6

> 1 cup heavy cream
> 1 cup whole milk
> ¼ teaspoon ground nutmeg
> ¼ teaspoon white pepper
> 4 large russet (Idaho) potatoes, peeled and thinly sliced
> 1 large white onion, very thinly sliced
> 3 tablespoons flour (all-purpose, or Wondra brand)
> ¼ cup (½ stick) chilled butter, cut into bits

1. Preheat the oven to 400°F. Grease a 9 x 13-inch glass baking dish, or other casserole.
2. Heat the cream and milk together in a saucepan. Stir in the nutmeg and white pepper. Bring just to a boil, then remove the pan from the heat.
3. Layer one-third of the sliced potatoes in the bottom of the baking dish or casserole. Cover with a layer of half the sliced onions. Season with salt and pepper and sprinkle 2 tablespoons of the flour over the onions. Dot with half the butter. Repeat with another one-third of the potatoes and all the remaining onions. Season with salt and pepper, then add the remaining flour and butter. Top with the rest of the sliced potatoes.
4. Slowly pour the warm cream mixture evenly over the potatoes and onions. Cover loosely with foil and bake for 30 minutes. Remove the foil, brush the top of the casserole with additional butter, and continue to bake, uncovered, until the top of the casserole is browned and the potatoes are tender, about 25 minutes.

For Roasted Garlic Cheddar Scalloped Potato Gratin:

Add 1 ½ cups (total) of grated Cheddar cheese, flavored with roasted garlic—such as Vermont's Cabot brand—to the recipe above. Divide the cheese in half and add along with the onion layers.

For Gruyère Scalloped Potato Gratin:

Add 1 teaspoon of minced garlic to the cream mixture in Step 2 above. Also, use 1 cup (total) of grated Gruyère or Emmenthaler cheese in the casserole, added in 2 layers, along with the onions.

Potato Latkes with Apple a[...]
Onion Chutney

makes a dozen latkes

Serve MOM's Apple and Onion Chutney (see Index) and a bowl of sour cream alongside these potato latkes.

5 medium Yukon Gold potatoes, peeled and grated
3 eggs
1 medium white onion, very thinly sliced
2 tablespoon minced flat-leaf parsley
2 tablespoons flour
1 ½ teaspoons salt
¼ teaspoon freshly ground black pepper
vegetable oil, for frying

1. Drain the grated potatoes and pat them dry between paper towels.
2. In a mixing bowl, beat the eggs, then add the potatoes and all the remaining ingredients. Toss to combine.
3. Heat a few tablespoons of oil in a large skillet or on a griddle. Drop a heaping ¼ cup of the batter into the hot pan to form each latke. Fry until dark golden brown and crisp on both sides. Serve immediately.

Mushroom Bread Pudding

STREET & CO., PORTLAND

serves 8

Chef Abby Harmon serves small slices of this rich, savory pudding next to a salad of field greens dressed with a tart vinaigrette as a first course. In larger portions, it makes a great side dish for roasted beef or poultry. You can use standard button mushrooms or a combination of portobellos, shiitakes, or chanterelles, if you can find them. Use any wild or specialty mushrooms you like.

This pudding is baked in a water bath, or *bain marie*, so be sure the baking dish you use for the pudding will fit inside a slightly larger one.

12 ounces fresh mushrooms, brushed clean and very coarsely chopped
¼ cup olive oil
2 teaspoons minced fresh thyme leaves, or 1 teaspoon dried
¼ teaspoon salt
¼ teaspoon freshly ground black pepper
8 eggs
4 cups cream
¾ cup finely grated Parmesan cheese
6 cups cubed French bread, crusts removed
1 medium roasted red bell pepper, peeled, seeded, and diced (see Index)

1. Preheat the oven to 450°F. Toss the mushrooms with the olive oil, thyme, salt, and pepper. Spread them on a baking sheet and roast for 10 to 15 minutes, or until golden brown. Remove the pan from the oven and let cool while you make the custard.
2. In a large mixing bowl, whisk together the eggs and cream. Stir in the cheese, bread cubes, and roasted red pepper. When the mushrooms are cool, toss them into the mixture. Cover and let the mixture rest for about 1 hour so that the custard is completely absorbed by the bread. (The pudding can be prepared a day in advance to this point.)
3. Preheat the oven to 350°F. Bring a large kettle of water to a boil for the water bath. Spread the pudding into a 9 x 13-inch glass baking dish and cover tightly with foil. Place the baking dish inside a large roasting pan, then place both on the oven rack. Carefully pour the boiling water into the larger pan so that it reaches about halfway up the sides of the glass baking dish.
4. Bake the pudding for 1 ½ to 2 hours, or until the custard is firm. Carefully lift the baking dish from the water bath and set the pudding aside to cool for 10 minutes before slicing it into individual servings.

Roasted Garlic Flans

STREET & CO., PORTLAND

These savory custards are nestled in a bed of tart greens as a first course at Street & Co. They are baked in a water bath, or *bain marie*—a simple procedure that's easy to master.

4 large heads of garlic
2 tablespoons olive oil
3 cups heavy cream
1 tablespoon minced shallots
¼ cup finely grated Parmesan cheese
2 whole eggs plus 1 additional egg yolk

1. Roast the garlic: Preheat the oven to 375°F. Remove most of the papery outer skins from the garlic heads and put them in a baking dish. Drizzle with the olive oil and roast for about 15 to 20 minutes, until the garlic is very soft and the cloves will easily squeeze out of their skins. (Reserve the oil for use in a vinaigrette for the salad that will accompany the flans.) Squeeze out all the garlic, purée it, and set aside. You should have about ½ cup.

2. In a saucepan, heat the cream with the shallots and grated cheese, whisking constantly, until it begins to steam, but do not boil. Remove the pan from the heat and allow the mixture to cool a bit. Pour the mixture through a fine-mesh strainer to remove the solids and any lumps, then whisk in the puréed garlic.

3. In a mixing bowl, beat the eggs, then whisk in the warm cream mixture a little at a time.

4. Reset the oven temperature to 350°F. Have ready a large kettle of boiling water. Place 8 individual ramekins inside a larger roasting pan. Fill each ramekin with about ½ cup of the custard mixture, then place the pan on the oven rack. Pour the hot water into the pan until it reaches halfway up the sides of the ramekins. Cover the pan with foil and bake for about 1 hour, or until the flans are set but still jiggle a bit in the centers.

5. Remove the flans from the water bath and cool to room temperature. When ready to serve, run a small knife around the edge of each flan, invert the ramekin onto a salad plate, and allow the flan to slide out. Serve beside a green salad dressed with a tart vinaigrette made with the oil from the roasted garlic (see Index).

Cheese Spaetzle

THOMASTON CAFÉ, THOMASTON

serves 4

Spaetzle is the German take on pasta. It makes a comforting side dish with almost any meal. Serve it with chicken, beef, or veal, or add it to soups and stews. It's a wonderful partner for any gravy or sauce. To serve spaetzle on its own, you can fry it in butter, along with a little minced onion, until golden brown.

There are many techniques for shaping spaetzle dough before dropping it into the pot. This old-fashioned method may be the simplest.

> 1 cup all-purpose flour
> 1 egg
> ½ cup water
> ½ teaspoon salt
> ¼ teaspoon freshly ground pepper
> ¼ teaspoon ground nutmeg
> 2 tablespoons grated Parmesan cheese

1. Have ready a large pot of boiling, salted water.
2. Mix all ingredients together to make a stiff batter. Let rest for 15 to 20 minutes, or cover and refrigerate until you are ready to cook the spaetzle.
3. Spread the batter into a long narrow strip over a cutting board, using a knife or a baker's spatula, until it is about ¼ inch thick. Cut small strips of the batter in quick succession, then drop all the spaetzle into the boiling pot.

   Note: The spaetzle should be of uneven sizes and shapes, so no need to be too cautious.

4. When the spaetzle come to the surface of the boiling water, reduce the heat and continue simmering for 2 to 3 minutes.
5. Strain well and toss with melted butter before serving.

Creative Coastal Cooking

Braised Red Cabbage

LOMPOC CAFÉ, BAR HARBOR

serves 6

"In the fall, we serve locally made sausages on a bed of this cabbage with stone-ground mustard on the side, and it is one of our biggest sellers. It would also be very good with pork loin roast or chops."

—CHEF LISE DESROCHERS

2 tablespoons olive oil
1 tablespoon whole mustard seeds
1 medium red onion, thinly sliced (about 1 ½ cups)
2 Granny Smith apples, peeled, cored, and sliced
2 tablespoons brown sugar
2 tablespoons balsamic vinegar
1 head red cabbage, cored and thinly sliced
1 cup white wine
½ teaspoon salt
½ teaspoon freshly ground black pepper

In large skillet or Dutch oven, heat the oil over medium heat. Add the mustard seeds and stir until they start to pop. Add the onion and apples and stir for 2 to 3 minutes. Add the remaining ingredients and cook for 15 minutes, tossing the mixture until the cabbage is crisp-tender.

Sweet Corn Fritters

10–12 fritters

3 or 4 ears fresh sweet corn (3 cups kernels sliced off the cob)
3 eggs
½ cup whole milk or cream
1 cup flour
1 cup cornmeal
1 teaspoon baking powder
½ teaspoon salt
¼ teaspoon freshly ground black pepper
6 tablespoons melted butter
1 red bell pepper, seeded and finely diced
1 fresh jalapeño pepper, seeded and minced
1 cup finely chopped scallions (white part and 3 inches green)
1 teaspoon minced fresh garlic
vegetable or canola oil, for frying

1. Put half the sweet corn kernels and 1 egg in the bowl of a food processor and purée. Transfer the mixture to a mixing bowl.
2. Stir in the milk. Add all the dry ingredients and mix well.
3. Fold in all the remaining ingredients.
4. Heat 3 tablespoons of oil in a large skillet. When the oil is very hot, ladle in ½ cup of batter for each fritter. Fry like pancakes, turning once, until nicely browned on both sides. Add more oil as needed to fry the batch. Serve with MOM's Red Pepper Mayonnaise (see Index).

Easy Dumplings

COURTESY THE AUTHOR

makes 8 dumplings

Amaze your friends with these incredibly light and fluffy dumplings—truly an heirloom recipe and classic comfort food. Steam them over a pot of Lompoc Café's Burgundy Beef Stew (see Index).

1 cup flour
2 teaspoons baking powder
½ teaspoon salt
½ cup buttermilk or whole milk
2 tablespoons canola or vegetable oil

1. Toss the dry ingredients together in a mixing bowl with a spatula.
2. In a small bowl, whisk together the buttermilk and oil until blended. Add the mixture to the dry ingredients with a few turns of the spatula.
3. Drop the batter by heaping tablespoons onto the surface of a simmering stew or soup.
4. Cover the pan with a tight-fitting lid and cook for about 12 minutes, until the dumplings have nearly tripled in size but remain glossy and moist.

"Trust Me" Couscous Cakes

CAFÉ MIRANDA, ROCKLAND

makes 8 cakes

These cakes are crusty on the outside and creamy on the inside—a great vehicle for stews and sauces.

"This started when we were living in St. George, Maine, about a twenty-minute ride from Café Miranda. It was a Sunday morning. We had the paper, champagne, each other, and no food. Except, that is, for some leftover couscous, frozen spinach, eggs, and cheese. We have served thousands of these in hundreds of guises. These are simple sautéed couscous cakes that have one thousand uses. Trust me."

—KERRY ALTIERO, OWNER, CAFÉ MIRANDA

5 eggs
2 cups prepared instant couscous (plain, unseasoned type)
½ cup grated Romano or Parmesan cheese
6 large fresh basil leaves, slivered
2 ounces chopped frozen spinach, well drained (or the same amount of
    cooked fresh)
a pinch of salt and a grind of fresh black pepper
canola or vegetable oil, for frying (about ½ cup)

1. In a mixing bowl, whisk the eggs until light. Add the couscous, cheese, basil, spinach, salt, and pepper. Fold the mixture until blended. Cover and let rest for about 1 hour as the mixture sets and thickens a bit.
2. When ready to make the cakes, heat the oil in a heavy skillet until very hot. Scoop the couscous mixture with an ice cream scoop or a large spoon. Quickly form the mixture into ¾-inch-thick patties, dropping them into the hot pan as you go.
3. Fry, turning once, until golden and crusty on both sides.

Some of Those One Thousand Uses

- Under any spicy meat- or bean-based stew
- Served with diced tomato, cucumber, yogurt, lemon, and parsley
- Alongside Stewed Lentils (see Index), served with chutney and yogurt
- With black beans, salsa, sour cream, and cilantro
- With a salad of arugula or frisée greens, dressed with fresh lemon and olive oil
- With any lamb dish, especially lamb curry, or lamb stew seasoned with rosemary
- As a base for eggs Benedict
- Floating in a rich, garlicky chicken stock with chickpeas, lemon, and parsley

Saffron Rice, or Jay's Golden Love

LOCAL 188, PORTLAND

serves 6

3–5 tablespoons olive oil
1 red bell pepper, seeded and diced
1 green pepper, seeded and diced
1 medium Spanish onion, diced
1 tablespoon fresh minced garlic
2 minced shallots
3 cups medium-grain white rice
1 teaspoon saffron threads, crushed
1 teaspoon salt
½ teaspoon freshly ground black pepper
4 ½–5 cups boiling water

1. In a large pot with a tight-fitting lid, heat 3 tablespoons of the olive oil. Add the red and green peppers, onion, garlic, and shallots. Sauté over low heat until the onion is translucent and the vegetables are softened. (Do not brown the mixture.)
2. Add the rice, saffron, salt, and pepper, and toss with the vegetables and oil, adding another tablespoon or two of oil, if needed, to coat the rice. Sauté the mixture for 3 minutes.
3. In another pan or kettle, bring the water to a boil. Add 4 ½ cups of water to the rice, stir once, and cover. Cook for 15 minutes.
4. Taste-test the rice for doneness. Add a bit more boiling water if needed, then cover and cook for another 3 to 5 minutes, or until tender but still firm.
5. Fluff the rice with a large fork or spatula and serve.

Wild Rice Pancakes

CHERIE'S, KENNEBUNK

a big batch—serves 8–10

These are savory pancakes to serve alongside any roasted poultry dish with a good sauce or gravy. This recipe makes at least 30 pancakes, but can easily be cut in half. Allow 3 per guest.

2 cups whole wheat flour
1 tablespoon baking powder
1 teaspoon salt
2 cups cooked wild rice
2 eggs, separated
2 cups whole milk
2 tablespoons fresh-squeezed lemon juice
4–6 tablespoons butter

1. Toss the dry ingredients and the rice together in a mixing bowl.
2. In another bowl, whisk the egg yolks, milk, and lemon juice. Mix with the rice mixture to make a batter.
3. Beat the egg whites until stiff and fold into the batter.
4. Begin by heating 2 tablespoons of the butter in a skillet. Drop the batter in by heaping tablespoons and brown on both sides, turning once. Remove the browned pancakes to a warm platter. Add butter as needed to fry all the pancakes.

Creative Coastal Cooking

Cranberry-Pecan Wild Rice Pilaf

CHERIE'S, KENNEBUNK

serves 4–6

Serve this pilaf with any roasted poultry or pork dish.

2 tablespoons butter
¾ cup chopped onion
¾ cup chopped celery
2 ¾ cups water
¼ cup wild rice
1 cup brown rice
¾ cup dried cranberries
½ cup chopped pecans, lightly toasted
¼ cup chopped fresh parsley
¾ teaspoon poultry seasoning blend (such as Bell's brand) or dried sage
salt and freshly ground black pepper to taste

1. Melt the butter in a saucepan with a tight-fitting lid. Add the onion and celery and sauté for about 5 minutes.
2. Add the water to the pan and bring to a boil. Add the wild rice, cover, and simmer for 10 minutes. Add the brown rice and return the pot to a simmer. Cover and cook for another 45 minutes, or until the rice is tender but still chewy. Add additional water, a tablespoon at a time, if needed.
3. When the rice is done, toss with the remaining ingredients and season to taste with salt and pepper.

Primo's Creamy Polenta

PRIMO, ROCKLAND

serves 4

Creamy polenta is a comforting side dish with any meat entrée that has a savory sauce or gravy. Try this with Primo's Braised Short Ribs of Beef (see Index).

2 cups whole milk
½ teaspoon minced fresh garlic
⅔ cup quick-cooking polenta
1 tablespoon butter
salt and green Tabasco to taste

1. Combine the milk and garlic in a medium saucepan and bring almost to a boil over high heat.
2. Slowly add the polenta, stirring constantly. Cook for 6 to 8 minutes, or until the mixture thickens to a porridge-like consistency.
3. Swirl in the butter. Season to taste and simmer a bit longer for a thicker consistency, or add additional milk to thin the mixture, as desired.

Melissa Kelly's Polenta Variations

Add to the basic polenta recipe:

- Mashed sweet potatoes
- Sautéed sweet corn and bell peppers
- Roasted garlic, Parmesan cheese, and chopped fresh herbs
- …anything you want; let your creative juices flow!

Chapter 6

Chefs' Entrées

SEAFOOD, CHICKEN, STEWS, PASTAS,
CASSEROLES, MEAT LOAF, AND
LOTS OF POT ROAST

At Rockland Harbor

Grilled Salmon with Maple-Ginger Glaze

CAFÉ THIS WAY, BAR HARBOR

serves 4

Use this glaze on salmon grilled indoors or out, or broil the salmon in a preheated oven, brushed with plenty of glaze.

¾ cup maple syrup
1 tablespoon minced fresh gingerroot
3 tablespoons soy sauce
4 salmon fillets, 8 ounces each

1. Simmer the maple syrup, ginger, and soy sauce together, stirring, for 10 minutes.
2. Grill the salmon for about 5 minutes per side, until done but still moist in the middle, while basting generously with the glaze.

Creative Coastal Cooking

Baked Atlantic Salmon with Green Garlic

PRIMO, ROCKLAND

serves 6

Use freshly picked stalks of green garlic for this light but flavorful salmon preparation. If green garlic is unavailable, substitute 3 large leeks or a bunch of scallions, using both the white and tender green parts. Serve this fish with a simple rice pilaf to absorb the delicious juices.

> 6 sheets parchment paper, each about 10 x 12 inches
> 6 salmon fillets (6 ounces each)
> 6–8 stalks green garlic, thinly sliced
> 6 tablespoons white wine
> 2 tablespoons olive oil
> 3 tablespoons butter, chilled
> 1 cup finely chopped garden herbs (combination of chervil, parsley, chives, and tarragon)
> salt and freshly ground black pepper to taste

1. Preheat the oven to 400°F.
2. For each fillet, fold a piece of parchment paper in half, and cut a heart shape from each sheet about 3 inches wider than the salmon fillets. Open the "hearts" and place each fillet on one side.
3. Divide the green garlic (or leeks, or scallions) among the fillets, along with the wine and olive oil. Top each fillet with ½ tablespoon of butter and sprinkle generously with the fresh herbs. Lightly season each fillet with salt and pepper. Fold the edges of the parchment paper several times to tightly seal up the packets.
4. Place the packets on a baking sheet and bake for 12 to 15 minutes, until they are puffed and slightly browned. Remove them from the oven and open carefully, allowing the steam to safely escape. Place the salmon and cooking juices on individual dinner plates and serve immediately.

Cornmeal-Crusted Cod with Cajun Tartar Sauce

CAFÉ THIS WAY, BAR HARBOR

serves 4

¼ cup vegetable or peanut oil
1 cup flour
4 eggs, beaten
1 cup cornmeal
4 fresh cod or haddock fillets (8 ounces each)
lemon wedges to garnish

1. Preheat the oven to 350°F. Have ready a baking sheet large enough to hold all the fish. Heat the vegetable oil in a heavy skillet.
2. Place the flour, eggs, and cornmeal in three separate shallow bowls. Dredge each piece of fish first in the flour, then the eggs, and then the cornmeal, coating thoroughly each time.
3. Place the fish in the hot skillet as you go. Fry each for 2 to 3 minutes per side, then transfer to the baking sheet.
4. Finish the dish by baking the fish until cooked through, about 12 minutes. Serve with Cajun Tartar Sauce and lemon wedges on the side.

Cajun Tartar Sauce

1 cup prepared mayonnaise
1 tablespoon drained capers
1 tablespoon drained green peppercorns
2 tablespoons pickle relish
a dash of hot sauce
1–2 tablespoons Cajun seasoning mix or All-Purpose Smoky Spice Blend (see Index)

Mix all the ingredients together, adding Cajun seasoning (or Smoky Spice Blend) to taste. Cover and chill before serving.

Potato-Crusted Halibut with Roasted Garlic Butter

CAFÉ THIS WAY, BAR HARBOR

serves 4

For the Roasted Garlic Butter:

12 cloves peeled garlic
1 tablespoon olive oil
½ cup butter, softened

For the halibut:

4 tablespoons prepared Dijon mustard
4 halibut fillets, 8 ounces each
1 cup peeled, grated russet potatoes
3–4 tablespoons vegetable oil

1. Preheat the oven to 350°F. In a small baking dish, drizzle the garlic cloves with 1 tablespoon olive oil. Cover tightly with foil and bake for 20 minutes, until the cloves as very soft. Let the garlic cool, then blend it into softened butter and set aside.
2. Spread 1 tablespoon of mustard over the top of each fish fillet. Press grated potatoes into the mustard to coat the fish.
3. Heat the vegetable oil in a heavy skillet. Place the fish fillets, potato-crusted-side down, in the oil and cook over medium-high heat until the potatoes begin to brown and crisp, about 2 to 3 minutes. Turn the fish and cook for 2 minutes more, then transfer the fillets to a baking sheet and bake at 350°F until the fish is cooked through, about 10 minutes.
4. To serve, place each fillet on a dinner plate and spread generously with Roasted Garlic Butter.

Gray Sole Fillets with Shrimp Mousse and Lemon Cream Sauce

BURNING TREE, BAR HARBOR

serves 4

1 cup peeled raw Maine shrimp
1 egg white
⅓ cup plus 1 tablespoon heavy or whipping cream
¼ teaspoon salt
4 skinless gray sole fillets (7–8 ounces each)
¼ cup water
¼ cup dry white wine
1 tablespoon snipped fresh dill weed, for garnish

1. For the shrimp mousse, place the shrimp, egg white, cream, and salt in a food processor and purée. Cover and refrigerate for 1 hour.
2. Preheat the oven to 450°F. Lay the fish fillets out on a flat work surface. Spread the chilled mousse over the fish, leaving the edges uncoated. Carefully roll up each fillet and secure with 2 or 3 toothpicks. (The mousse may begin to come out at the sides—simply press it back into the rolled fillet.)
3. Place the rolls in a baking dish, pour in the water and wine, and cover tightly with foil. Bake for 13 minutes, until the fish is opaque. Remove the toothpicks and transfer the rolls to serving plates. Spoon on Lemon Cream Sauce and garnish with fresh dill.

Lemon Cream Sauce for Fish

1 cup heavy or whipping cream
2 tablespoons dry white wine
2 tablespoons fresh lemon juice, or more to taste

In a small skillet over medium-high heat, simmer the cream, wine, and lemon juice until reduced and thickened. Season to taste with additional lemon juice—the sauce should be very tart.

Grilled Tuna with Sautéed Apples and Smoked Shrimp

CAFÉ THIS WAY, BAR HARBOR

serves 4

¼ cup (½ stick) butter
¾ cup honey
1 Granny Smith apple, peeled and slivered
8 ounces smoked shrimp
4 fresh tuna steaks (8 ounces each)

1. Melt the butter in a nonstick skillet. Add the honey, apple, and smoked shrimp and sauté until the apple is softened and golden brown.
2. Meanwhile grill the tuna (indoors or out) for 2 to 4 minutes per side for medium rare, or at least 5 minutes per side to cook through.
3. Place the hot tuna steaks on individual dinner plates and top with the sauce.

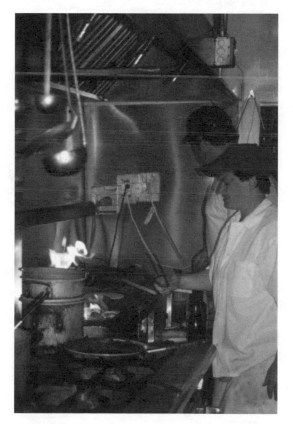

Chef Julie Harris in the kitchen, Café This Way

Fish Medina

LOMPOC CAFÉ, BAR HARBOR

serves 4

The flavors here are just a tad exotic—sweet and tangy, salty and sour. This recipe works well with any mild, flaky white fish. The sauce is also great served over char-grilled or pan-seared fish such as swordfish or halibut.

> 1 tablespoon olive oil
> 1 cup chopped onion
> ¼ cup finely chopped celery
> ½ teaspoon minced garlic (or more to taste)
> 1 ¼ cups ripe tomatoes, seeded and diced (or well-drained canned
>   plum tomatoes)
> ¼ cup pitted green olives
> 2 tablespoons golden raisins
> 1 tablespoon pine nuts
> 1 tablespoon capers, drained
> 2 pounds fresh cod or haddock fillets

1. Preheat the oven to 375°F. Mix all the ingredients—except the fish—in a saucepan and simmer for 10 minutes over medium heat.
2. Arrange the fish in an ovenproof baking dish, top with the sauce, and bake for 12 to 15 minutes, or until the fish is firm. Serve the fillets topped with pan juices and lemon wedges.

Pan-Fried Trout 188

LOCAL 188, PORTLAND

serves 2

> 3 tablespoons olive oil
> 2 boned trout fillets (skin-on, 6–8 ounces each)
> ½ cup milk
> 1 cup dry bread crumbs seasoned with salt and pepper
> ¼ cup (½ stick) soft butter
> 1 tablespoon minced shallots
> 1 teaspoon minced garlic
> 1 thinly sliced portobello mushroom, stems and gills removed
> 10 thin spears fresh asparagus
> ¼ cup dry white wine
> lemon wedges, for garnish

1. Heat the olive oil in a large skillet over high heat. Have ready 2 dinner plates for the trout.

2. When the oil is hot, quickly dip the trout in the milk, then in the bread crumbs. Place the trout skinless-side down in the skillet and cook for about 2 minutes, until just brown. Turn carefully, cook for 2 minutes more, then transfer the trout to the dinner plates.
3. Pour off the excess oil from the skillet. Add the butter, shallots, garlic, mushroom slices, asparagus, and wine. Sauté for just 2 to 3 minutes to sear the vegetables and deglaze the skillet.
4. To serve, place the vegetables around the trout and drizzle with the wine-and-butter sauce. Garnish with lemon wedges.

Pasta with Tuna Bolognese Sauce

STREET & CO., PORTLAND

serves 4 as an entrée (6 as a first course)

Choose a wide-noodle pasta such as fettuccine, tagliatelle, or pappardelle to go with this rich sauce from chef Abby Harmon.

12 ounces fresh tuna steak or fillet, all skin and bones removed
2 tablespoons olive oil
1 tablespoon minced fresh garlic
1 tablespoon chopped anchovies
½ cup minced onion
½ cup minced red bell pepper
½ cup minced celery
1 ½ teaspoons crushed red pepper flakes
1 cup dry red wine
¾ cup heavy cream
1 teaspoon ground nutmeg
2 cups Basic Marinara Sauce (see Index), or your preferred version of marinara
1 pound dried pasta
grated Pecorino Romano or Parmesan cheese

1. Cut the tuna into large chunks and pulse in a food processor until it is coarsely ground. (Or coarsely grind the tuna in a meat grinder.) Set aside.
2. Heat the olive oil in a large skillet. Add the garlic and anchovies and sauté for 3 minutes. Add the onion, bell pepper, celery, and red pepper flakes and sauté until the onion is soft, about 10 minutes.
3. Add the ground tuna and sauté until browned. Add the wine and simmer, uncovered, for 10 minutes to reduce the mixture. Add the cream and nutmeg and simmer for an additional 10 minutes, stirring often.
4. Add the prepared marinara sauce and bring to a simmer.
5. Prepare and drain the pasta. Put the pasta in serving bowls, top with the sauce, and serve with plenty of grated cheese on the side.

Hot Crab Pasta Toss

CAFÉ MIRANDA, ROCKLAND

serves 4

A rich summer pasta dish, the result of Kerry Altiero's favorite way to cook: Check out what's on hand and come up with a creative mix of flavors and textures—then toss it up.

The sauce base for this dish is Café Miranda's Buttermilk Roasted Garlic Dressing. Have four pasta bowls ready for serving. Kerry likes a cold Fumé Blanc with this one.

¼ cup extra-virgin olive oil
1 teaspoon hot pepper flakes (or more to taste)
¼ cup (about 1 bunch) snipped fresh chives, plus extra for garnish
¾ cup Café Miranda's Buttermilk Roasted Garlic Dressing (see Index)
8 ounces crabmeat, precooked and thoroughly shelled
½ cup shredded radicchio lettuce
1 cup packed, torn fresh spinach leaves
1 pound fresh pasta such as spaghetti or linguine (dried works, too)
salt and freshly ground black pepper to taste

1. In a large, wide salad bowl, whisk together the olive oil, pepper flakes, chives, and dressing. Fold in the crabmeat, radicchio, and spinach. Set aside while you cook the pasta.
2. Cook the pasta until al dente, reserving about ½ cup of the pasta cooking water.
3. Drain the hot pasta quickly, then toss it with the crabmeat mixture. Let rest a minute or two while the spinach and lettuce wilt a bit. Add the reserved hot pasta water 1 teaspoon at a time, if needed, to keep the dish a little saucy. Season with salt and pepper to taste and garnish with snipped chives.

Chef Kerry Altiero

Creative Coastal Cooking

Lemony Wheat Fettuccine with Sea Scallops

CAFÉ MIRANDA, ROCKLAND

serves 4

Café Miranda produces its own homemade egg pasta, which is sold at food shops in the Rockland area. Their chewy whole wheat fettuccine inspired this dish. The sauce has a classic "brown butter" base. You heat the butter until it colors, but turn the heat off quickly so it doesn't burn. Once you've got all the ingredients prepped, this dish will be ready in minutes.

> 1 pound fresh whole wheat fettuccine, or ½ pound dried
> ½ cup (1 stick) butter
> 12 ounces large sea scallops with any tough edges trimmed away
>   (called "sweet meats" in Maine)
> 6–8 scallions, sliced, including all the white and 3 inches of the greens
> 2 tablespoons extra-virgin olive oil
> salt and freshly ground black pepper to taste
> 1 fresh lemon, cut into wedges
> grated Asiago cheese (optional)

1. Bring a pot of salted water to a boil and begin cooking the pasta according to directions.

   Note: Fresh pasta will cook more quickly than dried, so work fast.

2. In a wide, heavy skillet, heat the butter over a high flame until very hot. Place the scallops in the pan; as the butter browns, the scallops will sear to a rich brown color in about 2 minutes per side. Remove the scallops to a warm serving bowl.

   Note: Once the butter turns brown, turn off the heat and continue cooking in the hot skillet.

3. Drain the pasta when it's al dente and set aside.
4. Add the scallions to the skillet, cooking just until their color intensifies, about 2 minutes. (Return the skillet to medium heat if needed at this point.) Return the scallops to the skillet and add the pasta and olive oil. Toss the mixture and season to taste with salt and pepper, then tong it into individual pasta bowls. Serve with grated Asiago, if you like, and lemons on the side.

Lemony Wheat Fettuccine Variation

Instead of sea scallops, use 6 ounces of fresh crabmeat and 3 ounces of prosciutto cut into small julienne strips. Add both along with the scallions and cook for just 2 to 3 minutes total before tossing with the cooked pasta.

Fish Cakes Four Ways

Basic Salmon Cakes
STREET & CO., PORTLAND

8 cakes

1 ½ pounds salmon fillets, all bones, skin, and dark meat removed
3 egg yolks
3 tablespoons prepared dried bread crumbs (unseasoned type)
½ cup minced onion
1 tablespoon minced fresh garlic
3 tablespoons capers, drained and minced
¼ cup prepared Dijon mustard
2 tablespoons snipped fresh dill weed, or 2 teaspoons dried
1 teaspoon salt
¼ teaspoon cayenne
¼ teaspoon white pepper
vegetable oil, for frying

1. Cut the salmon into large chunks. Place the fish in a food processor and pulse for a few times to coarsely grind it. Reserve.
2. In a mixing bowl, beat the egg yolks with the bread crumbs. Add all the remaining ingredients, including the salmon, and toss to combine. Shape the mixture into 8 patties and place them on a platter lined with waxed paper. (Cover and refrigerate, if not frying the cakes immediately.)
3. Heat the vegetable oil in a heavy (or nonstick) skillet. When the pan is hot, add the patties and fry, turning once, until browned on both sides, about 8 minutes total.

Asian Flavor Tuna-Salmon Sausage
CAFÉ THIS WAY, BAR HARBOR

makes 8 patties

8 cloves garlic
1-inch piece peeled fresh gingerroot, chopped
8 ounces fresh tuna, skin and bones removed
8 ounces fresh salmon, skin, dark meat, and bones removed
1 cup sesame seeds
¼ cup peanut or vegetable oil
soy sauce, pickled ginger, and wasabi, as accompaniments

1. In a food processor, purée the garlic and ginger.

2. Cut the tuna and salmon into 1-inch cubes and place in the food processor with the garlic-ginger mixture. Pulse a few times until the fish is coarsely ground into small bits.
3. Divide the mixture into 8 round patties. Heat the oil in a large skillet.
4. Dip the patties in the sesame seeds to lightly coat both sides. Fry over medium heat until crisp and brown, about 3 minutes per side. Serve with the soy sauce, pickled ginger, and wasabi on the side.

Haddock–Sweet Potato Cakes

MARKET ON MAIN, ROCKLAND

serves 4

For the haddock:

1 tablespoon fresh-squeezed lemon juice
1 tablespoon minced fresh garlic
1 tablespoon prepared Dijon mustard
1 pound skinless, boneless haddock fillet

Preheat the oven to 400°F. Combine the lemon juice, garlic, and mustard and spread evenly over the haddock. Bake until cooked through, about 8 to 10 minutes.

Set the fish aside to cool.

For the roasted vegetables and sweet potatoes:

2 tablespoons butter
¼ cup olive oil
1 ½ cups chopped onion
1 cup chopped celery
1 cup thinly sliced leeks
1 pound peeled sweet potatoes, diced
salt and freshly ground black pepper

1. Melt the butter and combine it with 2 tablespoons of the olive oil, the onion, celery, and leeks. Spread the mixture in a baking dish and place in the oven.
2. Toss the diced sweet potatoes with the remaining 2 tablespoons of olive oil, season with salt and pepper, and place them in a separate baking dish.
3. Bake the vegetables and the potatoes until tender. Set aside to cool.

For the fish cakes:

1 ½ cups fine fresh bread crumbs
1 ½ cups mayonnaise
2 eggs
1 tablespoon finely grated fresh gingerroot
⅛ teaspoon cayenne, or more to taste
1 tablespoon prepared Dijon mustard
1 tablespoon minced garlic
canola oil, for frying

1. Toss the fish cake ingredients with the roasted vegetables and sweet potatoes. Flake the haddock into the mixture and toss lightly to combine. Chill the mixture for 1 hour before frying.
2. Heat 2 tablespoons canola oil in a large skillet. Form the fish cake mixture into 8 patties and fry over medium-high heat until golden brown, about 3 or 4 minutes per side. Serve with Lemon-Caper Tartar Sauce (see Index).

Crispy Crab and Shrimp Cakes

LOMPOC CAFÉ, BAR HARBOR

makes 8 cakes

"These crab cakes fly out of the restaurant whenever we make them. They're a perfect dish for company because you can prepare the cakes ahead of time and just pop them in a hot frying pan at the last minute. They are easy, but elegant. We use fresh Maine crab (of course!), but Maryland or California crabs work just as well."

—PATTI SAVOIE, OWNER, LOMPOC CAFÉ

For the crab cakes:

½ cup mayonnaise, plus ¼ cup additional if needed
1 cup unseasoned dry bread crumbs
1 pound crabmeat, picked over for any shell bits
½ pound cooked shrimp, coarsely chopped
¼ cup finely minced red onion
½ cup finely minced celery
1 teaspoon prepared whole-grain mustard
¼ teaspoon salt
¼ teaspoon freshly ground black pepper
1 teaspoon fresh lemon juice
2 tablespoons minced fresh parsley

For frying:

1 additional cup unseasoned dry bread crumbs
1 tablespoon butter
1 tablespoon olive oil

1. Starting with ½ cup of the mayonnaise, place all the ingredients for the crab cakes in a large bowl. Toss the mixture lightly with your hands until just blended. It should hold together in moist patties. If it seems too dry, add the additional mayonnaise.
2. Form eight 4-inch-wide patties, coating each with additional bread crumbs. If you are not frying the cakes immediately, place them on a platter lined with waxed paper, cover with plastic wrap, and refrigerate.
3. To fry the crab cakes, heat the butter and oil together in a skillet over medium-high heat. When the skillet is hot, add the cakes and fry for 3 to 4 minutes per side, until crisp and golden brown. Serve with lemon wedges and any seafood sauce you prefer.

Abby's Biscuit Top Clam Pie

STREET & CO., PORTLAND

serves 6

The preferred type of clam for this recipe is the New England longneck steamer, but littlenecks, or quahogs, could also be used. Chef Abby Harmon says there's really nothing like fresh clams for this dish, but if they are not available, try a quart of good-quality frozen clams packed in their juices, often found in specialty seafood shops. If you go with frozen clams, be sure to use 2 cups of bottled clam juice for added flavor, instead of the water called for in the recipe.

Serve this pie with a salad of sharp, chewy greens such as dandelion or escarole, dressed with a tart vinaigrette.

For the filling:

4 ounces salt pork, coarsely chopped
2 cups finely chopped onion
1 large clove garlic, minced
2 medium russet or Yukon Gold potatoes, peeled and diced
2 cups water (or bottled clam juice)
2 tablespoons all-purpose flour
2 tablespoons soft butter
1 quart fresh, shucked clams in their juices
½ cup heavy cream
1 teaspoon Tabasco sauce, or more to taste
salt and pepper to taste

For the topping:

4 cups all-purpose flour
2 tablespoons baking powder
1 teaspoon baking soda
1 teaspoon salt
⅔ cup soft butter, plus 2 tablespoons melted butter, set aside
1 ½ cups buttermilk
1 tablespoon snipped fresh dill
1 tablespoon chopped fresh thyme leaves

1. Grease a large rectangular baking dish or a casserole and preheat the oven to 375°F.
2. In a large skillet, fry the salt pork until crisp to render the fat. Remove the pork scraps and discard them. Add the onion and garlic to the fat and sauté until soft and golden. Add the potatoes along with 2 cups water and simmer until the potatoes are fork-tender, about 10 or 12 minutes.
3. In a small bowl, blend the flour and soft butter until smooth and set aside.
4. To the simmering potato mixture, add the clams along with their juices, then whisk in the flour-butter mixture and continue to simmer over low heat. The sauce should thicken to a light gravylike consistency in about 5 minutes. Whisk in the cream and the Tabasco. Season to taste with salt and pepper and

remove from heat. Pour the mixture into the greased baking dish and set aside while you prepare the biscuit top.

5. Place the flour, baking powder, soda, and salt in a large mixing bowl and toss with a spatula to blend. Cut in the soft butter with a large fork or pastry blender, or work with your fingers, until the mixture resembles small peas. Add the buttermilk and herbs and blend quickly until the dough pulls away from the sides of the bowl.

6. Lightly dust your hands with flour, gather the dough from the bowl and place it on a flour-dusted work surface. Knead it lightly for 2 minutes. Roll out the dough to a 1-inch thickness, cut out 8 biscuits, and arrange them on top of the clam mixture. Brush with the reserved melted butter. Bake until the biscuits are light golden brown, about 20 to 25 minutes.

Wild Maine Mussels

THOMASTON CAFÉ, THOMASTON

serves 4 as an appetizer (2 as a main course)

1 ½ cups dry white wine
4 cloves garlic, coarsely chopped
½ cup sliced onion
12 whole black peppercorns
¼ cup torn fresh basil leaves, or 1 tablespoon dried basil
4 pounds live Maine mussels

1. Place the wine, garlic, onion, peppercorns, and basil in a large nonreactive (nonaluminum) stockpot with a tight-fitting lid. Stir the ingredients to combine, bring to a boil, and simmer for 2 minutes. Add the mussels, cover the pot, and steam the mussels for about 5 minutes, or until all the shells have opened.

2. To serve, pour the mussels and their broth into individual soup bowls or a big tureen for the center of the table. Serve with buttery garlic bread.

Scrubbing and Debearding Live Mussels

Wild Maine mussels have a stronger and more hearty flavor than the farm-raised variety, but they need more cleaning and soaking. To clean mussels well, put them in a large bowl of cold salted water and let them soak for 1 hour. Scrub them with a brush under cold running water. Discard any that have broken shells or don't close when tapped. Wait to debeard the mussels until just before you cook them.

Street & Co. Bouillabaisse

STREET & CO., PORTLAND

serves 10–12

"Bouillabaisse is the fisherman's stew of southern France. It is said to be made from whatever was left over from the day's catch. In the little villages of Provence, the dish is traditionally served in three stages—first comes the broth, then a platter of steamed fish, then the sautéed vegetables, fragrant and golden from the saffron. Rouille is the sweet pepper sauce used to enhance each course. I find that it is just as wonderful to eat everything in one bowl together. That is how my mother would serve it in her home in the small coastal town of Cutler, Maine."

—CHEF ABBY HARMON

This is a lush, classic bouillabaisse recipe. It is not difficult to make, but it takes time to prepare this dish from scratch—and it's worth the effort. Choose a day when you can cook at your leisure, or make the fish stock and rouille sauce a day or two in advance.

Abby recommends a dry French white or rosé wine to accompany the stew, along with plenty of French bread.

For the rouille:

3 roasted red peppers, peeled and seeded (see Index)
3 large cloves fresh garlic
¼ cup toasted fresh bread crumbs
¼ cup olive oil
a pinch of cayenne
a pinch of saffron
1–2 tablespoons water
salt to taste

Place all the rouille ingredients in a blender or food processor and pulse until smooth. Cover and reserve until ready to serve the bouillabaisse.

For the bouillabaisse:

3 tablespoons olive oil
2 tablespoons minced fresh garlic
2 tablespoons minced anchovies
2 tablespoons minced shallots
1 leek (white part and 1 inch green), rinsed and thinly sliced
2 carrots, peeled and diced
2 stalks celery, diced
¼ cup Pernod
½ cup dry white wine
2 tablespoons saffron threads
1 can (12 ounces) tomatoes, chopped
5 cups fish stock (see Index)
2 medium redskin or Yukon Gold potatoes, unpeeled, cut into 1-inch cubes
2 bulbs fresh fennel, trimmed and thinly sliced

1 pound live mussels, scrubbed and debearded (see Index)
1 pound Down East mahogany clams
1 pound boneless, skinless monkfish fillets, coarsely chopped
1 pound boneless, skinless cod fillets, coarsely chopped
1 pound prepared lobster meat, coarsely chopped
6 ounces cleaned squid, cut into ¼-inch rings
8 ounces crabmeat, picked over for shells

1. In a stockpot large enough to hold all the bouillabaisse ingredients, heat the olive oil and sauté the garlic, anchovies, and shallots for 5 minutes. Add the leeks, carrots, celery, Pernod, white wine, and saffron and simmer for 5 minutes.
2. Add the tomatoes, fish stock, potatoes, and fennel. Bring the mixture to a boil, reduce the heat, and simmer, uncovered, for 15 minutes more.
3. Add the mussels, clams, monkfish, and cod to the pot. Cover and bring to a boil. Steam for about 10 minutes, until the mussels and clams are open and the fish fillets are firm and flaky.
4. Add the lobster, squid, and crabmeat to the pot. Cover and steam for 2 or 3 minutes longer.
5. To serve, ladle the bouillabaisse into big soup or pasta bowls, with plenty of broth, fish, and shellfish in each serving. Serve the rouille in a separate bowl as an accompaniment to be spooned into each serving to taste.

Cioppino Lompoc

LOMPOC CAFÉ, BAR HARBOR

serves 8–10

This stew is a mix of shellfish and meaty fish fillets in a rich tomato-wine broth. Use one type of fish, or a combination. The stew is especially aromatic made with fresh herbs from the garden. Serve it with buttery garlic bread and a green salad.

2 tablespoons olive oil
3 cups chopped onion
1 large red bell pepper, seeded and chopped
1 tablespoon minced fresh garlic
2 cups sliced mushrooms
1 can (28 ounces) crushed tomatoes
1 can (28 ounces) whole plum tomatoes, drained and coarsely chopped
3 cups fish stock (see Index) or prepared clam juice
1 cup dry white wine
2 bay leaves
2 tablespoons chopped fresh basil, or 1 ½ teaspoons dried
2 teaspoons minced fresh oregano leaves, or 1 teaspoon dried
2 teaspoons minced fresh thyme leaves, or 1 teaspoon dried
1 ½ teaspoons fennel seeds, lightly crushed
2 cups prepared chickpeas, well drained
12 ounces fresh fish fillets (see Note)
8 ounces scallops (cut in half if very large)
8 ounces medium-sized shrimp, peeled and deveined
1 pound live mussels, scrubbed and debearded (see Index)
salt and pepper to taste
sugar to taste
chopped fresh parley, for garnish

1. In a large soup or stockpot, heat the oil over medium heat. Add the onion, bell pepper, and garlic and sauté until soft. Add the mushrooms and cook for 5 minutes more.
2. Add all the tomatoes, fish stock (or clam juice), wine, herbs, and chick peas. Bring the stew to a boil, then lower the heat and simmer uncovered for 30 minutes.
3. Add the fish fillets and simmer for 5 minutes, then add the scallops, shrimp, and mussels. Raise the heat if needed to keep the stew at a simmer while gently pushing the seafood under the liquids. Continue to cook for 5 to 7 minutes, until the mussels have opened.
4. Using a large fork or wooden spoon, gently break up the fish fillets into meaty chunks as you stir the stew. Season to taste with salt and pepper, and add sugar—½ teaspoon at a time—if the tomato flavor is too tart. Serve in wide soup or pasta bowls, garnished with chopped parsley.

Note: For a milder stew, use cod, haddock, or sea bass; for a stronger fish flavor, use swordfish, salmon, or bluefish.

Lavender Roasted Chicken

BURNING TREE, BAR HARBOR

At Burning Tree, Allison Martin uses partially boned breasts of free-range chicken for this recipe. The lavender flowers infuse the butter with just a hint of their aromatic perfume. She serves the chicken over a bed of steamed Swiss chard, with roasted new potatoes and baby carrots from the garden alongside. Lavender Butter can be used to prepare any cut of chicken, or a whole, roasted bird.

For Lavender Butter

1 pound (4 sticks) unsalted butter, at room temperature
zest and juice of 1 lemon
2 teaspoons snipped fresh thyme leaves
2 ½ tablespoons fresh or dried organic lavender flowers (the small purple buds)

Fold the ingredients together to blend. Store in the refrigerator or freezer in an airtight container.

Lavender Roasted Chicken Breasts

serves 4

4 plump chicken breast halves, with skin
10 tablespoons chilled Lavender Butter
salt and freshly ground black pepper
1 cup chicken stock (see Index)

1. Preheat the oven to 475°F.
2. Stuff 2 tablespoons of Lavender Butter under the skin of each chicken breast. Place the chicken in a roasting pan. Season lightly with salt and black pepper.

   Note: New potatoes and carrots, coated lightly with olive oil, can be added to the roasting pan with the chicken at this point.

3. Roast the chicken to an internal temperature of 150°F. (If you're roasting dark meat, cook to an internal temperature of 175°F.)
4. When the chicken is done, remove it to a platter. Deglaze the roasting pan with 2 tablespoons of additional Lavender Butter and the chicken stock. Simmer for 5 minutes to reduce. Serve the pan sauce drizzled over the chicken and vegetables.

Creative Coastal Cooking

Whole Lavender Roasted Chicken

serves 2-4

1 plump roasting chicken (4 ½–5 pounds)
10 tablespoons Lavender Butter
salt and freshly ground black pepper

1. Preheat the oven to 450°F. Rinse the chicken inside and out. Pat dry.
2. Loosen the breast skin of the chicken and stuff with 6 tablespoons of the Lavender Butter. Season the entire chicken lightly with salt and black pepper.
3. Place the chicken on a rack in a shallow roasting pan and bake at 450°F for 10 minutes, then reduce the oven temperature to 350°F and roast for another 1 ½ hours. As the chicken roasts, baste every 20 minutes with additional Lavender Butter and pan drippings.
4. When the chicken is done, let it rest for at least 10 minutes before carving.

Citrus Roasted Chicken

MARKET ON MAIN, ROCKLAND

serves 2-4

1 plump roasting chicken (4–5 pounds)
⅓ cup olive oil
2 cloves garlic
juice of 1 lemon
¼ cup fresh-squeezed orange juice
½ teaspoon fennel seeds
1 teaspoon fresh rosemary, or ½ teaspoon dried
1 teaspoon fresh thyme, or ½ teaspoon dried
1 teaspoon dried marjoram
⅛ teaspoon cayenne
⅛ teaspoon black pepper
¾ teaspoon sea or kosher salt
1 medium yellow onion, quartered

1. Preheat the oven to 450°F. Rinse the chicken inside and out. Pat dry.
2. Place all the remaining ingredients—except the quartered onion—in a blender or food processor and combine.
3. Rub the chicken with the mixture, inside and out. Place the quartered onion inside the cavity, along with any leftover lemon and orange rinds. Loosely tie or truss the chicken.
4. Place the chicken on a rack in a shallow roasting pan and bake at 450°F for 10 minutes, then reduce the oven temperature to 350°F and roast for another 1 hour and 20 to 30 minutes. Let the chicken rest for at least 10 minutes before carving.

Cashew-Crusted Chicken with Sesame-Ginger Aioli

CAFÉ THIS WAY

serves 4–6

> 1 cup roasted, unsalted cashews
> 1 cup dry bread crumbs
> ¼ cup vegetable or canola oil
> 1 cup flour
> 4 eggs, beaten
> 8 boneless, skinless chicken breasts (about 4 ounces each)

1. For the cashew crust, pulse the cashews with the bread crumbs in a food processor to make a fine meal. Preheat the oven to 350°F. Have ready a lined or greased baking sheet large enough to hold all the chicken.
2. Heat the oil in a large skillet. Place the flour, cashew crust meal, and eggs in 3 separate shallow bowls.
3. Dredge each chicken breast first in the flour, then the eggs, and then the cashew crust meal, coating both sides of the chicken each time. Place the chicken in the hot oil as you go.
4. Lightly brown the chicken over medium-high heat, turning once, about 2 to 3 minutes per side. Place the browned chicken breasts on the baking sheet and finish in the oven for about 12 minutes, or until the chicken is cooked through. Serve hot, with Sesame-Ginger Aioli on the side.

Sesame-Ginger Aioli

makes about 1 ¾ cups

> Use this sauce with chicken or seafood dishes, grilled or fried.
> 10 cloves fresh garlic
> 1 inch peeled fresh gingerroot, chopped
> 1 cup prepared mayonnaise
> ¼ cup soy sauce
> ¼ cup toasted sesame seed oil
> 2 tablespoons toasted sesame seeds

1. In a food processor, purée the garlic and ginger together. Add the mayonnaise and soy sauce and pulse to blend.
2. With the motor running, slowly drizzle in the sesame oil to make a creamy emulsion.
3. Blend in the sesame seeds and serve in a small bowl as sauce for Cashew-Crusted Chicken.

Pine Nut Parmesan Crusted Chicken Breasts

MARKET ON MAIN, ROCKLAND

serves 4

Try some Spanish Romesco sauce with these fried chicken breasts (see Index).

2 cups fine fresh bread crumbs
½ cup pine nuts
½ cup grated Parmesan cheese
¼ cup chopped flat-leaf parsley
1 egg
¼ cup milk or cream
1 cup flour seasoned with 1 teaspoon each salt, black pepper, and paprika
4 boneless, skinless chicken breasts
¼ cup olive oil

1. Place the bread crumbs, pine nuts, grated cheese, and parsley in a food processor and pulse to combine, until the mixture resembles a coarse meal. Set aside in a shallow bowl.
2. Beat the egg with the milk. Place the seasoned flour in a shallow bowl. Dip each chicken breast in the seasoned flour, then the egg mixture, then coat with the bread crumb mixture. Place the chicken on a rack, cover loosely, and chill for at least 30 minutes before frying.
3. Heat the olive oil in a skillet. Fry the chicken breasts over medium-high heat until golden brown, about 5 minutes per side.

Creative Coastal Cooking

Chicken Baked in Chipotle Cream Sauce

LOMPOC CAFÉ, BAR HARBOR

serves 4–6

Monterey Jack and Chipotle Cream Sauce is a signature item at Lompoc—here's yet another way to use it. Serve this chicken and its delicious sauce with mashed potatoes or rice.

2 tablespoons olive oil
1 whole chicken (3–4 pounds), cut into 8 serving pieces
salt and freshly ground black pepper
2 cups Monterey Jack and Chipotle Cream Sauce (see Index)
1 cup grated Monterey Jack cheese
½ cup whole milk

1. Preheat the oven to 350°F. Heat the olive oil in an ovenproof skillet with a tight-fitting lid.
2. Rinse and pat the chicken dry. Season lightly with salt and pepper and sear the chicken over medium heat until the skins have turned golden brown. Remove the pan from the heat.
3. Bake the chicken, uncovered, for 30 minutes. Remove the pan from the oven and spread the Monterey Jack and Chipotle Cream Sauce evenly over the chicken pieces. Cover, return to the oven, and bake for an additional 10 minutes.
4. Remove the cover from the pan. Sprinkle each piece of chicken with 2 tablespoons of grated cheese. Bake, uncovered, until the cheese begins to brown, about 10 minutes.
5. Place the chicken on a serving platter and return the skillet to the stove top. Add the milk and whisk over low heat until the sauce is bubbly and smooth. Serve the sauce in a separate bowl or gravy boat.

Bar Harbor

Honey Bourbon Sauce and Spicy Pecans for Chicken or Pork

LOMPOC CAFÉ, BAR HARBOR

At the Lompoc, this sauce goes over grilled or pan-seared chicken breasts, or pork tenderloin or chops, topped with spicy pecans.

For the slurry:

1 cup chicken stock
¼ cup Wondra flour

Whisk together the stock and flour to make the slurry—the sauce thickener. Set aside.

For the Honey Bourbon Sauce:

1 ½ cups Vidalia onion, thinly sliced
2 tablespoons olive oil
1 cup fresh lemon juice
1 cup Jim Beam Kentucky Bourbon, or your preferred bourbon
1 cup honey
2 tablespoons tamari
1 tablespoon peeled and grated fresh gingerroot
1 tablespoon chopped fresh garlic
1 teaspoon salt
½ teaspoon freshly ground black pepper

1. Sauté the onion in the olive oil over medium-high heat until it begins to brown.
2. Add the remaining ingredients and bring to a boil. Simmer uncovered for 10 minutes.
3. Whisk in the slurry mixture, return to a boil, and continue to whisk for about 3 minutes more, or until the sauce is thick.

For the Spicy Pecans:

These are great on meat dishes topped with honey bourbon sauce, or as a snack on their own.

1 tablespoon canola oil
1 ½ cups pecan halves
1 ½ teaspoons chili powder (regular, chipotle, or adobo)
1/4 teaspoon cayenne, or more to taste
1 teaspoon salt
1 teaspoon sugar
1 teaspoon lemon juice

Preheat the oven to 400°F. Toss all the ingredients—except the lemon juice—on a rimmed baking sheet. Bake for 10 to 15 minutes, stirring quickly once or twice. Remove the pan from oven and sprinkle the pecans with the lemon juice. Toss until the juice is absorbed. Cool and store in an airtight container.

How to Cook a Christmas Goose...

Traditional Roasted Goose with Cherry Sauce

THOMASTON CAFÉ, THOMASTON

serves 4

"Where I come from in Germany, Christmas dinner without a goose is like Thanksgiving dinner in America without the turkey."

—HERBERT PETERS, CHEF-OWNER, THOMASTON CAFÉ

You may want to save the rendered goose fat from this recipe. Some consider it a delicacy and use it instead of cooking oil for frying or roasting potatoes.

1 goose (about 8–9 pounds)
1 kettle of boiling water
1 tablespoon salt
1 teaspoon freshly ground pepper
2 apples, unpeeled, cored and diced
1 cup pitted prunes
1 tablespoon dried rosemary (or 2 tablespoons fresh)
1 cup coarsely chopped onion
1 cup coarsely chopped carrots
1 cup coarsely chopped celery
additional water (about 2 cups) for the roasting pan

1. Preheat the oven to 400°F. Over a sink, carefully pour boiling water over the outside and inside of the goose—the skin will contract and the hot water will kill any possible bacteria. Pat dry.
2. Rub the salt and pepper into the bird, inside and out, then fill the cavities with the apple, prunes, and rosemary. Truss the goose as you would any poultry.
3. Put the chopped vegetables in a shallow roasting pan and place the goose, breast-side up, on top.
4. Roast the goose until it begins to smell good and render its fat, about 30 minutes. Carefully take the pan from the oven and remove the goose to a platter. Pour off as much of the rendered fat as possible, then return the bird to the pan. Reduce the oven to 325°F.
5. Add 2 cups of water to the pan and continue roasting until the skin is crisp. The total roasting time should be about 2 ½ hours, or until the goose reaches an internal temperature of 165°F.
6. Remove the goose to a platter and cover loosely with foil.

For the cherry sauce:

2 cups water
¼ cup cornstarch
1 cup red wine
1 can or jar (16 ounces) pitted bing cherries in juice
2 tablespoons brandy
salt and pepper to taste

1. Pour the water over the browned vegetables in the roasting pan and bring to a simmer on top of the stove. Scrape the pan to lift and dissolve all the good browned bits (this will give your sauce color and flavor). Cook for about 5 minutes to reduce.
2. Strain this mixture through a wire mesh into a saucepan. Remove 1 cup of the mixture and whisk in the cornstarch until smooth. Return this mixture to the saucepan.
3. Add the wine, cherries (juice and all), and brandy and bring to a simmer. Stir until the sauce is thick, then season to taste with salt and pepper.
4. Carve the goose as you would a turkey and serve with the sauce.

Braised Short Ribs of Beef

PRIMO, ROCKLAND

serves 6

6 meaty short ribs of beef, bone-in (about 14 ounces each; 5–6 pounds total)

For the marinade:

1 chopped onion
6 cloves minced fresh garlic
4 whole sprigs thyme
2 cups hearty red wine
2 bay leaves
½ cup red wine vinegar
1 whole black peppercorns

For braising:

1 tablespoon olive oil
salt and freshly ground black pepper
1 chopped onion
2 stalks celery, diced
3 carrots, peeled and thick-sliced
3 tablespoons tomato paste
3 cups rich beef or veal stock (see Index)

1. Mix together the marinade ingredients in a bowl large enough to hold all the short ribs. Add the ribs, cover, and marinate for at least 2 hours, or overnight in the refrigerator.
2. Remove the ribs from the bowl, reserving the marinade. Heat the olive oil in a large ovenproof pot or Dutch oven. Season the ribs lightly with salt and pepper and sear them until golden brown on all sides. Remove the ribs from the pot and reserve.
3. Add the onion, celery, and carrots to the pot and lightly brown them. Add the tomato paste and cook for 5 minutes more. Add all the reserved marinade to the pot and bring to a boil, stirring to deglaze the pot. Simmer, uncovered, until the mixture is reduced by one-third. Meanwhile, preheat the oven to 325°F.
4. Add the stock to the pot and bring to a boil. Add the ribs, cover, and bake for 1 ½ to 2 hours, or until very tender.
5. Remove the ribs from the pot and set aside. For the sauce, strain and degrease the braising liquid. Serve the ribs with mashed potatoes, with the sauce on the side in a gravy boat.

Pot Roast Three Ways

Mediterranean Pot Roast

MARKET ON MAIN, ROCKLAND

serves 8

¼ cup mild paprika
2 teaspoons salt
1 teaspoon freshly ground black pepper
2 tablespoons dried thyme
¼ cup ground coriander
1 boneless chuck roast (4–5 pounds), cut 2 inches thick
3 tablespoons olive oil
1 ½ cups onion cut into 1-inch chunks
1 cup celery cut into 1-inch chunks
1 cup thick-sliced carrots
3 cups tomato purée
1 cup orange juice
1 orange, cut in half
1 cup pitted black olives, cut in half
½ cup chopped flat-leaf parsley, for garnish

1. Blend together the paprika, salt, pepper, thyme, and coriander. Rub the mixture over the entire surface of the roast. Wrap the roast in plenty of plastic wrap. Refrigerate for at least 4 hours, or overnight.
2. In a large cast-iron Dutch oven, heat 2 tablespoons of the olive oil. Add the roast and thoroughly sear it on all sides. Remove the roast to a platter. Add the remaining tablespoon of oil to the pot and sauté the vegetables until soft, about 10 minutes.
3. Return the roast to the pot and add the tomato purée, orange juice, and orange halves. Add enough water to the pot to reach the surface of the roast. Bring to a simmer, cover, and cook for at least 3 hours, until the beef is very tender.
4. Remove the roast from the pot. Slice or pull it into large chunks, discarding any fatty chunks or connective tissue. Remove 3 cups of liquid and vegetable bits from the pot and purée in a food processor. Return the meat and purée to the pot, along with the olives.
5. Simmer for another 10 to 15 minutes. Serve the chunks of the roast over mashed potatoes, with plenty of sauce from the pot, garnished with the chopped parsley.

Creative Coastal Cooking

Pot Roast with Wine and Peppers

COURTESY THE AUTHOR

serves 8

1 boneless chuck roast (4–5 pounds), cut 2 inches thick
2 tablespoons paprika
1 teaspoon salt
1 teaspoon freshly ground black pepper
3 tablespoons olive oil
2 cups red wine—Cabernet or Burgundy
1 can (8 ounces) tomato sauce
1 red bell pepper, seeded and coarsely chopped
3 fresh jalapeño peppers, seeded and minced
3 cloves chopped fresh garlic
3 carrots, peeled and thickly sliced
2 large onions, peeled and cut into wedges
1–2 cups beef stock (see Index)

1. Preheat the oven to 350°F. Trim excess fat from the roast and season it on all sides with paprika, salt, and pepper.
2. Heat the olive oil in an ovenproof casserole or Dutch oven just large enough to hold the roast. Sear the roast on all sides until well browned.
3. Add the wine to the pot and simmer, uncovered, until reduced by one-third. Add the tomato sauce, peppers, garlic, and carrots to the pot. Finish by layering all the onion wedges over the roast. Cover the pot and bake for at least 4 hours, until the meat is completely tender.
4. To serve, lift the roast from the pot and place on a serving platter. It should fall apart into tender chunks.
5. Strain the pot liquids from the solids, reserving both. Degrease the liquids, season with additional salt to taste, and serve as a sauce on the side. Arrange the vegetables around the roast. Serve with mashed or roasted potatoes.

Asian-Flavor Pot Roast

serves 6

Serve this over plain, steamed Asian-style rice, such as basmati, jasmine, or Thai sticky rice.

3 tablespoons peanut oil
1 thick-cut rump roast (about 3 pounds)
½ cup dry sherry
2 tablespoons chopped fresh gingerroot
2 tablespoons chopped fresh garlic
¼ cup soy sauce
1 cup beef stock (see Index)
2 tablespoons molasses
¼ cup brown sugar
1 tablespoon Chinese chili paste in oil
2 tablespoon Thai red chili sauce (sambal sauce)
1 tablespoon Thai red curry paste
1 teaspoon cardamom
5 whole star anise
2 large white onions, peeled and slivered
2 tablespoons cornstarch blended with ¼ cup sherry
½ cup chopped scallions, white and green parts, for garnish
¼ cup chopped fresh cilantro, for garnish

1. Preheat the oven to 350°F. Heat the peanut oil in an ovenproof casserole or Dutch oven just large enough to hold the roast. Sear the roast on all sides until well browned.
2. Remove the roast to a platter. Deglaze the pot with the ½ cup sherry and simmer to reduce by half.
3. Add all the remaining ingredients—except the cornstarch-sherry mixture—to the pot. Cover and bake for 3 ½ to 4 hours, or until the roast is completely tender.
4. Pull the roast from the pot and set aside on a deep serving platter or a wide serving bowl. Pull away any excess fat or connective tissue and discard. Slice the meat against the grain.
5. Strain the liquid from the pot and degrease it to make the sauce (discard the solids). Reheat the liquid and whisk in the cornstarch-sherry mixture. Simmer until the sauce has the consistency of a thin gravy or glaze. Season to taste with additional soy sauce or sherry.
6. To serve, pour the hot sauce over the meat, then garnish with the chopped scallions and cilantro.

Burgundy Beef Stew

LOMPOC CAFÉ, BAR HARBOR

makes a big batch—serves 12

This is a classic beef stew recipe that results in plenty of rich gravy for serving with Easy Dumplings or a warm slice of Lompoc's Porter Ale Bread (see Index). Seasoning the finished stew with a spoonful of Smoky Spice Blend gives it a little added heat.

- 6 tablespoons olive oil
- 4 cups coarsely chopped onion
- 1 cup coarsely chopped celery
- 1 cup thickly sliced carrots
- 1 ½ tablespoons chopped garlic
- 3 pounds stewing beef (Lompoc Café uses London broil, trimmed of fat and cut into 1-inch cubes)
- ½ cup flour
- 1 pound very coarsely chopped mushrooms (halved or whole if they're small)
- 3 cups Burgundy (or any dry red wine)
- 8 cups beef stock, canned or scratch-made (see Index)
- 3 bay leaves
- 1 teaspoon dried thyme
- 1 teaspoon sage
- 1 teaspoon tarragon
- 5 cups potatoes cut into 1-inch cubes (any kind, peeled or unpeeled)
- salt and freshly ground black pepper to taste
- 1 cup peas (optional)
- 1 tablespoon All-Purpose Smoky Spice Blend (see Index)
- about 3 tablespoons Wondra brand flour, to thicken

1. In a large soup pot or Dutch oven, heat 2 tablespoons of the olive oil and sauté the onion, celery, carrots, and garlic until soft, about 10 minutes. Remove the vegetables from the pot and reserve.
2. Put the cubed beef in a large paper or plastic bag, sprinkle in the flour, and shake until the meat is coated. In the soup pot, heat 2 more tablespoons of the olive oil. Brown the meat in batches, adding the final 2 tablespoons of oil as needed and being careful to turn the meat so that it browns on all sides.
3. Add the mushrooms to the beef and sauté until they release their juices. Add the wine and bring to a simmer, scraping up any brown bits on the bottom or sides of the pot.
4. Add the stock, bay leaves, and herbs. Bring the stew to a simmer and cook, covered, for about 1 hour and 20 minutes, or until the beef is very tender.
5. Add the potatoes, then cover and simmer until they are tender, about 15 to 20 minutes. Season the stew with salt and pepper to taste. Add the peas, if using, and the Smoky Spice Blend.
6. To thicken, stir the stew as it simmers while you sprinkle in the Wondra a little at a time, until the stew reaches the desired consistency. Remove the bay leaves and serve.

Traditional Sauerbraten

THOMASTON CAFÉ, THOMASTON

serves 6

Herbert Peters grew up in Germany—here's his family recipe for authentic, homemade sauerbraten. Serve it with Herbert's Cheese Spaetzle (see Index).

1 boneless bottom beef round or chuck roast (4–5 pounds)
2 cups cider vinegar
1 cup water
1 cup red wine
1 large onion, thinly sliced
2 carrots, peeled and sliced
1 clove minced fresh garlic
1 bay leaf
12 whole black peppercorns
3 whole cloves
1 teaspoon sugar
3 tablespoons olive oil
¼ cup soft butter blended with ¼ cup flour
salt, freshly ground black pepper, and sugar to taste
finely chopped dill pickle, parsley, and sour cream, for garnish

1. Trim the roast of excess fat and set it aside while you prepare the marinade.
2. Combine the vinegar, water, wine, onion, carrots, garlic, bay leaf, peppercorns, cloves, and sugar in a nonreactive (nonaluminum) stockpot or Dutch oven. Bring just to a boil.
3. Place the roast in the marinade. Cover and refrigerate for at least 48 hours, turning the meat several times each day.
4. When ready to prepare the sauerbraten, remove the roast from the marinade. Pat dry the surface of the roast, then season it lightly with salt and pepper. Strain the marinade liquids from the solids, reserving both.
5. Clean the stockpot and add the olive oil. Heat the oil and sear the roast on all sides, until evenly browned. Add the reserved solids from the marinade, plus 2 cups of the liquids. Bring the pot to a simmer, cover, and cook, basting with additional marinade liquid as needed, for 2 ½ hours, until very tender.
6. When the meat is done, remove it to a cutting board and slice it against the grain. Arrange the meat on a serving platter, cover, and keep warm.
7. Strain the cooking liquid and return it to the pot, along with any remaining marinade liquid. Bring to a simmer and deglaze, scraping away any browned bits on the bottom and sides of the pot. Whisk in the butter-flour paste and simmer for 5 minutes longer, or until the sauce thickens. Season the sauce to taste with salt, pepper, and sugar.
8. Pour the sauce over the meat and garnish with chopped pickle, parsley, and sour cream.

Spinach and Mushroom Stuffed Meat Loaf

CHERIE'S, KENNEBUNK

serves 8–10

For the meat loaf:

3 pounds ground beef
3 eggs
1 ½ cups dry bread crumbs
1 tablespoon Worcestershire sauce
1 teaspoon dried basil
1 teaspoon dried oregano
1 teaspoon salt
½ teaspoon freshly ground black pepper
¼ cup grated Parmesan cheese

For the filling:

1 tablespoon olive oil
2 teaspoons minced fresh garlic
1 medium shallot, peeled and minced
2 cups sliced mushrooms
¼ cup Burgundy or other dry red wine
4 cups chopped fresh spinach leaves
salt and pepper to taste
1 cup grated sharp Cheddar cheese

1. Preheat the oven to 350°F. Have ready a large loaf pan or oval casserole dish, lightly greased.
2. Place all the meat loaf ingredients in a large mixing bowl and mix with a spatula, or toss together with your hands, until well blended.
3. Heat the olive oil in a skillet, add the garlic and shallot, and sauté until soft.
4. Add the mushrooms and sauté until they release their liquids. Add the wine and cook until it has evaporated and the mushrooms begin to brown. Add the spinach and toss with the mushrooms just until wilted. Season to taste with salt and pepper. Remove the pan from the heat and set aside.
5. Lay a generous length of plastic wrap over a cutting board. Form the meat loaf mixture into a large rectangle, about 9 x 12 inches. Place the filling down the middle of the meat loaf and top with the grated cheese. Lifting the plastic wrap, fold the meat loaf over the filling and seal the ends.
6. Place the meat loaf in a the loaf pan or casserole, cover loosely with foil, and bake for 1 hour. Remove the meat loaf from the oven, pour off the fat to degrease, then cover and let rest about 10 minutes before slicing.

MOM's Meat Loaf

MARKET ON MAIN, ROCKLAND

makes 1 big meat loaf

3 tablespoons butter
1 cup finely chopped onion
½ cup finely chopped celery
1 carrot, peeled and finely chopped
1 ½ cups fresh bread cubes
1 cup cream
2 pounds ground beef
1 pound ground pork
3 eggs
1 tablespoon minced fresh garlic
2 tablespoons prepared Dijon mustard
2 tablespoons Worcestershire sauce
1 tablespoon dried oregano
½ cup ketchup
1 ½ teaspoons salt
½ teaspoon freshly ground black pepper

For the glaze:

1 cup ketchup mixed with 2 tablespoons prepared horseradish

1. Preheat the oven to 350°F. Line a large, shallow roasting pan with waxed or parchment paper.
2. Melt the butter in a skillet. Add the onion, celery, and carrot and cook over low heat until the vegetables are soft, about 10 minutes. Set aside to cool.
3. In a large mixing bowl, soak the bread cubes in the cream until saturated. Add the cooked vegetables and all the remaining ingredients and toss the mixture with a wide spatula, or with your hands, to combine.
4. Mound the meat loaf into an oval shape, about 3 inches thick, in the roasting pan. Bake for 30 minutes, then brush on the glaze and bake for another 30 minutes.

Creative Coastal Cooking

Armenian Lamb-Stuffed Peppers

CAFÉ MIRANDA, ROCKLAND

serves 4

This dish has pungent curry, juicy lamb, and plenty of heat from a generous measure of cayenne. The "sort of kefta" meatball mix, as chef Kerry Altiero likes to call it, is a versatile stuffing. It can be formed into meatballs or into patties for char-grilling, as well as stuffed into peppers, as described here.

Cindy McGuril, an accomplished weaver of Armenian heritage who lives in Rockland, gave Kerry the basic kefta concept, and he ran with it.

For the hot curry blend:

2 teaspoons good-quality curry powder
½ teaspoon cayenne, more or less, to taste
½ teaspoon ground cumin
½ teaspoon ground coriander

For the yogurt sauce:

1 cup plain yogurt
2 tablespoons fresh lemon juice
1 teaspoon ground coriander
salt and pepper to taste

For the kefta:

1 ½ pounds ground lamb
⅓ cup minced fresh parsley, plus 2 tablespoons set aside for garnish
3–4 large cloves garlic, minced
a dash of salt and pepper
3–4 unblemished poblano peppers
olive oil for frying, about 2–3 tablespoons
1 cup Basic Marinara Sauce (see Index)

1. In a small dish, assemble the hot curry blend and set aside. Preheat the oven to 375°F.
2. Make the yogurt sauce, cover, and refrigerate.
3. Toss the lamb with the parsley, garlic, salt, and pepper to make the kefta.
4. Halve the peppers lengthwise and remove the seeds. Stuff as many halves as needed to use up all the kefta.
5. In a heavy skillet, heat the olive oil. Carefully place the peppers in the pan and cook over high heat for about 5 minutes, or until they begin to brown along the bottom. (No need to turn them.)
6. Reduce the heat and add the marinara sauce, pouring it over the peppers to coat. Cover and bake for 20 to 25 minutes. The peppers should remain tender-crisp.
7. To serve, divide the peppers on serving plates, spooning on the marinara sauce and then a tablespoon of the yogurt sauce. Dust the whole plate generously with the hot curry blend. (The more curry, the hotter the dish.) Garnish with chopped parsley.

Mustard-Crusted Lamb Chops with Tomato-Mint Jam

PRIMO, ROCKLAND

serves 4

12 (¾-inch-thick) lamb chops, excess fat and silverskin tissues trimmed away
2 eggs
2 teaspoons prepared coarse-grain mustard
1 teaspoon prepared Dijon mustard
salt and freshly ground black pepper
1 cup fine bread crumbs
3 cloves minced fresh garlic
2 tablespoons chopped fresh parsley
4 tablespoons olive oil

1. Preheat the oven to 400°F.
2. Lightly season the lamb with salt and pepper. Let the meat rest at room temperature for at least 30 minutes before cooking.
3. Whisk the eggs with the mustards and season with salt and pepper to taste. In a separate, shallow dish, toss together the bread crumbs with the garlic, parsley, and 2 tablespoons of the oil. Season the mixture with additional salt and pepper.
4. Heat the remaining 2 tablespoons of olive oil in a large skillet and sear the lamb chops over high heat until browned on all sides. Set them aside to cool for 5 minutes.
5. Brush each chop liberally with the egg-mustard mixture, then dredge in the bread crumb mixture. Place the chops on a baking sheet and bake for 7 to 10 minutes for a medium-rare center. Serve with Tomato-Mint Jam (see below).

Melissa's Tomato-Mint Jam

enough for 12 lamb chops

2 tablespoons vegetable oil
1 cup diced white onion
3 cloves minced fresh garlic
2 fresh jalapeño peppers, seeded and minced
2 tablespoons minced fresh gingerroot
1 cup brown sugar
1 cup red wine vinegar
¼ teaspoon cayenne
12 plum tomatoes, seeded and diced
¼ cup chopped fresh mint leaves
salt and freshly ground black pepper to taste

Creative Coastal Cooking

1. Heat the oil in a saucepan. Add the onion and cook for 3 to 4 minutes, stirring, over medium-high heat (do not brown). Add the garlic, jalapeños, and ginger. Cook for 3 minutes more.
2. Add the brown sugar, vinegar, and cayenne and bring to a boil. Add the diced tomatoes and cook, uncovered, until the liquid begins to evaporate and the mixture looks "jammy," about 25 minutes. Remove the pan from the heat and stir in the mint. Season to taste with salt and pepper. Cool to room temperature before serving.

Jerry's Inside-Out Blue Cheeseburgers

CAFÉ MIRANDA, ROCKLAND

serves 4

It's a Café Miranda tradition to offer every staff member (and significant other) the meal of his or her choice at the start of every shift. Good policy, and a good source of new ideas. This one was invented on a whim by a five-year veteran of Miranda, Jerry Brooks of Union, Maine. For these burgers, opt for full-fat ground beef, not the lean stuff, for a juicy result. Miranda owner Kerry Altiero loves to cook outside the lines. Here's a new way to think about cheeseburgers.

8 ounces crumbled blue cheese
½ medium red onion, very thinly sliced
½ cup chopped fresh parsley
2 tablespoons fresh-squeezed lemon juice
3 tablespoons extra-virgin olive oil
½ teaspoon red pepper flakes (optional)
a generous grind of black pepper
salt to taste
1 pound ground beef
4 slabs crusty bread, grilled (see Note)

1. In a large mixing bowl, toss together the cheese, onion, parsley, olive oil, red pepper flakes (if using), black pepper, and salt. Set aside while you grill the burgers.
2. Shape the meat into four ¾-inch-thick patties. Pan-fry or grill the meat to the desired degree of doneness, about 3 minutes per side for medium rare.
3. When the burgers are done, put them in the bowl with the cheese mixture and toss as you would a salad, breaking up the burgers into large chunks. Serve immediately on buns or over grilled bread, pouring on any juices that remain in the bottom of the bowl.

Note: This burger mix can be served piled on traditional buns if you like, or served "open-face" on 1-inch-thick slabs of dense, crusty bread that have been brushed with olive oil and marked on the grill (outdoors) or lightly toasted (indoors).

Brown Rice and Mushroom Burgers

ROGUE RIVER CAFÉ, DAMARISCOTTA

makes 12 burgers

2 cups short-grain brown rice
4 cups water
1 tablespoon olive oil
⅔ cup finely chopped red onion
2 teaspoons minced fresh garlic
½ cup finely chopped red bell peppers
2 portobello mushrooms, stemmed and chopped
1 pound fresh spinach leaves, chopped
2 tablespoons chopped fresh basil
2 tablespoons chopped fresh parsley
2 teaspoons prepared Dijon mustard
2 tablespoon rice wine vinegar
½ cup toasted nuts (cashews, walnuts, almonds, or a mix)
1 cup fine fresh bread crumbs
salt and freshly ground black pepper to taste
olive oil, for frying

1. Bring the brown rice and water to a simmer. Cover and cook until the rice is tender. Spread it on a baking sheet, lined with waxed or parchment paper, to cool.
2. Heat the olive oil in a skillet and sauté the onion and garlic until soft, about 8 minutes. Add the peppers, mushrooms, spinach, basil, and parsley and sauté until the spinach has wilted and the peppers are tender. Transfer the mixture to a mixing bowl. Add the mustard, vinegar, nuts, and bread crumbs and toss to combine.
3. Place half the cooked rice in a food processor and pulse until it has an oatmeal-like texture. Add all the rice to the mixing bowl and toss again. Season with salt and pepper to taste.
4. To fry, heat additional olive oil in a skillet until hot. Form the mixture into patties, using ½ cup at a time. Fry until browned and crispy on both side.

Sicilian Spaghetti and Meatballs

MARKET ON MAIN, ROCKLAND

serves 6

Most cooks have a favorite version of marinara, so use your own in this recipe if you like. Canned tomatoes vary greatly in their degree of sweetness. Marinara, or any tomato-based sauce or soup, often benefits from the addition of a little sugar. Remember—the tomato is, after all, a fruit.

You will need:

1 batch Sicilian Meatballs
1 batch marinara sauce (at least 8 cups)
1 ½ pounds imported, dried Italian spaghetti
2 cups finely grated Pecorino Romano cheese

Sicilian Meatballs

makes about 14 meatballs

1 thick slice fresh Italian bread, crusts trimmed (about 1 cup torn bread bits)
⅔ cup whole milk
1 pound ground beef
8 ounces ground pork
8 ounces ground veal
1 tablespoon minced fresh garlic
½ cup chopped flat-leaf parsley
½ cup finely grated Pecorino Romano cheese
2 teaspoons dried oregano
½ teaspoon crushed red pepper flakes
1 tablespoon Worcestershire sauce
2 eggs, beaten
olive oil, for frying

1. In a large mixing bowl, stir together the bread and the milk. Allow the bread to absorb all the milk.
2. Add the meat and mix with the bread and milk, using a wide spatula or your hands.
3. Add all the remaining ingredients and toss lightly to combine.
4. Roll the mixture into meatballs about 2 inches in diameter. Cover and set aside until the marinara sauce is ready.

Basic Marinara Sauce

makes 8-10 cups

3 cans (28 ounces each) whole peeled Italian plum tomatoes
¼ cup olive oil
2 small carrots, peeled and finely chopped
2 stalks celery, finely chopped
2 tablespoons minced fresh garlic
3 tablespoons chopped fresh basil, or 2 teaspoons dried
2 teaspoons finely chopped fresh oregano leaves, or 1 teaspoon dried
1 teaspoon crushed red pepper flakes (optional)
½ cup dry red wine
salt, freshly ground black pepper, and sugar to taste
additional olive oil, for browning meatballs

1. Lift the tomatoes from the can juices with a fork and place them, in batches, in a food processor. Pulse three or four times to break them up into large pieces. Reserve the tomatoes. Strain 2 cups of the can juices and reserve. (Discard the remaining can juices or reserve them for another use.)
2. Heat the ¼ cup of oil in a large non-aluminum stockpot. Add the carrot and celery and cook over very low heat until soft, about 10 minutes. Add the garlic and cook for 3 minutes more. Do not brown the garlic.
3. Add the tomatoes, reserved tomato juices, basil, oregano, red pepper flakes (if using), and wine. Bring the sauce to a simmer and cook, uncovered, for 30 minutes, stirring often.
4. Season to taste with salt and pepper. If the sauce tastes too tart, add sugar a teaspoon at a time, to taste.

Assembling the Sicilian Spaghetti and Meatballs:

Heat 2 tablespoons of olive oil in a skillet. Brown the meatballs on all sides in batches. Lift them out of the skillet and carefully drop them into the simmering pot of marinara sauce. Once all the meatballs have been added to the pot, continue to simmer, uncovered, for an additional 30 minutes. Serve over hot spaghetti, cooked al dente, with plenty of grated Pecorino Romano on the side.

Greek Eggplant and Pasta Casserole

MARKET ON MAIN, ROCKLAND

serves 6–8

Here's a satisfying layered casserole from MOM. You can stir a pinch or two of cinnamon into the tomato sauce for an authentic Greek touch.

1 large eggplant, cut into ½-inch-thick slices
¼ cup olive oil
salt and freshly ground black pepper
3 eggs
1 cup heavy or whipping cream
1 cup half-and-half
8 ounces ricotta cheese
8 ounces crumbled feta cheese
2 teaspoons minced garlic
2 teaspoons dried oregano
½ teaspoon red pepper flakes
1 pound penne pasta, cooked al dente and drained
2 cups prepared tomato sauce (see Index)
3 tablespoons capers, drained
2 cups fine white bread crumbs
2 tablespoons chopped flat-leaf parsley
¼ cup melted butter

1. Preheat the oven to 400°F. Grease a 9 x 13-inch baking pan, or other large gratin or casserole dish.
2. Line a cookie sheet with waxed or parchment paper. Brush each slice of eggplant on both sides with olive oil. Season the slices with salt and pepper and bake, turning once, until soft and browned, about 20 minutes. Set aside to cool. Reduce the oven temperature to 350°F.
3. In a large mixing bowl, beat the eggs with the cream and half-and-half. Add the cheeses, garlic, oregano, and red pepper flakes and stir until smooth. Add the cooked pasta and toss the mixture until blended.
4. To assemble the casserole, put half the pasta mixture in the baking dish. Layer on half the roasted eggplant slices, then spread on all the tomato sauce. Sprinkle the capers evenly over the tomato. Follow with the rest of the pasta mixture, topped with the remaining eggplant.
5. Toss the bread crumbs with the parsley and melted butter. Season with salt and pepper, and sprinkle the mixture evenly over the casserole.
6. Cover with foil and bake for 45 minutes. Remove the foil and bake for an additional 15 to 20 minutes, until golden brown. Allow the casserole to cool for at least 15 minutes before serving.

Southwestern Tortilla Stack

LOMPOC CAFÉ, BAR HARBOR

serves 8–10

This casserole is the southwestern answer to lasagne. Corn tortillas serve as the "noodle" layers between lots of spicy sautéed vegetables and melted cheese. The basic recipe is vegetarian, but switching to the meaty version is easily done.

2 tablespoons vegetable oil, plus ½ cup for frying tortillas
2 cups chopped onion
1 cup shredded or diced carrots
2 red bell peppers, seeded and chopped
2 fresh jalapeño peppers, seeded and minced
2 teaspoons minced fresh garlic
1 ½ cups diced zucchini
3 cups corn kernels, cut fresh from the cob, or frozen
2 large ripe tomatoes, seeded and diced, or 2 cups canned tomatoes, drained and chopped
2 roasted poblano peppers, peeled, seeded, and diced (see Index), or ½ cup canned green chiles, drained
¼ teaspoon cayenne, or more to taste
½ teaspoon ground cumin
½ teaspoon dried oregano
1 teaspoon salt
½ teaspoon freshly ground black pepper
12 (6-inch) corn tortillas
3 cups grated Monterey Jack cheese
2 cups grated Cheddar cheese
4 eggs
2 cups sour cream
2 tablespoons minced fresh cilantro
Salsa Verde or Salsa Fresca (optional; see Index)

1. Heat 2 tablespoons of oil in a large skillet. Add the onion and cook until translucent. Add the carrots, red bell pepper, jalapeños, and garlic and sauté for 5 minutes more over medium-high heat.
2. Add the zucchini, corn, tomatoes, and green chiles. Bring to a simmer and cook, uncovered, for 5 minutes.
3. Stir in the cayenne, cumin, oregano, salt, and pepper. Remove the pan from the heat and set aside. Preheat the oven to 375°F and lightly oil a 9 x 13-inch baking dish, or other deep casserole.
4. In a small skillet, heat the remaining ½ cup of oil. Using tongs, dip each tortilla in the hot oil for a second or two, then remove quickly and drain on paper towels.
5. To assemble the casserole, spread half the vegetable mixture in the baking dish. Cover the vegetables with half the Monterey Jack and half the Cheddar. Top with an overlapping layer of 6 tortillas. Repeat the layers with all the remaining vegetables, the cheeses, and the last 6 tortillas.

Creative Coastal Cooking

6. In a mixing bowl, beat the eggs until light. Blend in the sour cream and cilantro until smooth. Pour the mixture evenly over the casserole. Bake for 30 to 40 minutes, or until the sour cream custard topping just begins to brown. Cool for at least 20 minutes before cutting into squares. Top with salsa, if desired.

Note: To lighten the fat content of this dish, chef Lise Derochers suggests that you can skip Step 4. Instead of frying the tortillas in hot oil, simply dip them in tomato juice to moisten them before building the casserole.

Meaty Southwestern Tortilla Stack

For the vegetable layer, omit the carrots and zucchini, and reduce the corn to 1 cup. In a separate skillet, brown 1 pound of crumbled sausage, drain off the rendered fat, and toss the cooked sausage with the sautéed vegetables. Proceed with the recipe as directed.

Spanish Beans and Rice

LOCAL 188, PORTLAND

serves 8

Local 188 offers this vegetarian version of Spanish Beans, but you can add the optional smoked ham for a meaty, and authentically Spanish, variation. Either way, serve these beans over a bed of Saffron Rice with some of Local 188's Mojo Sauce on the side for some added heat (see Index for recipes).

1 pound red or black beans
2 tablespoons olive oil
1 large Spanish onion, coarsely chopped
1 green pepper, seeded and diced
1 yellow pepper, seeded and diced
1 tablespoon minced fresh garlic
12 ounces smoked ham, diced (optional)
2 cups drained canned tomatoes, coarsely chopped
6–8 cups vegetable or chicken stock (see Index)
1 tablespoon chili powder
2 tablespoons minced fresh cilantro
salt and freshly ground black pepper to taste

1. Soak the beans overnight in plenty of cold water. Drain and rinse them.
2. Heat the olive oil in a soup pot. Add the onion, peppers, garlic, and ham (if using) and sauté until the vegetables are soft, about 10 minutes.
3. Add the beans, tomatoes, and 6 cups of the stock. Bring the mixture to a boil, reduce the heat, and simmer, partially covered, for about 1 ½ hours, or until the beans are tender, adding additional stock if needed to keep the beans moist.
4. When the beans are done, stir in the chili powder and cilantro. Season with salt and pepper to taste.

Chapter 7

Desserts Worth the Trip

CHEESECAKES AND COOKIES, PUDDINGS AND PIES

Evan Altiero at Café Miranda

Easy Chocolate Mousse

CAFÉ THIS WAY, BAR HARBOR

serves 4–6

2 cups semisweet chocolate chips
½ cup strong coffee or espresso
¼ cup liqueur, such as Kahlúa, Amaretto, or Frangelico
2 ½ cups heavy or whipping cream

1. Have ready 4 wineglasses or other dessert dishes (or 6, for smaller portions).
2. In a double boiler or heavy saucepan, melt the chocolate chips with the coffee and liqueur over low heat, stirring until smooth. Remove the pan from the heat and let cool to room temperature.
3. Whip 2 cups of the cream until it forms stiff peaks, then gently fold in the cooled chocolate mixture.
5. Spoon the mousse into the wineglasses, cover and chill for at least 2 hours before serving.
5. To serve, whip the remaining cream and spoon it on top of the mousse.

Note: Cooks who love making chocolate desserts should keep a jar of instant espresso on hand. Add a teaspoon or two, diluted in a tablespoon of hot water, to enhance the flavor of chocolate in almost any recipe. Ferrara brand is widely available in specialty markets and keeps indefinitely in the cupboard.

The Wonder Woman theme table for two at Café This Way

Lemon Parfait with Maine Blueberries

CAFÉ THIS WAY, BAR HARBOR

serves 4

> 1 jar (10 ounces) ready-made lemon card, or 1 ½ cups Scratch-Made Lemon Curd (see below)
> 2 cups whipping cream
> 1 cup fresh blueberries or other fresh, ripe berries

1. Have ready 4 wineglasses or other dessert dishes. Whisk the lemon curd until smooth in a large mixing bowl.
2. In another bowl, whip the cream until it forms stiff peaks. Gently fold the whipped cream into the lemon curd until just blended. Spoon the mixture into the wineglasses, cover, and refrigerate for at least 3 hours before serving, topped with berries.

Scratch-Made Lemon Curd

makes 3 cups

Lemon curd tastes like the tart filling in lemon meringue pie. For a proper "cream tea," the British spread it on split scones and top it with thick Devonshire cream, accompanied by a pot of freshly brewed hot tea, of course.

For Lemon Curd Tartlets, simply bake off tartlet shells using Basic Pie Dough Pastry (see Index). When the shells are cool, fill them with prepared lemon curd. Cover and chill the tartlets, then dust with powdered sugar just before serving.

> 10 egg yolks, lightly beaten
> 1 ½ cups sugar
> ¾ cup fresh-squeezed lemon juice, strained
> ¾ cup (1 ½ sticks) unsalted cold butter, chopped

1. In a saucepan over low heat, whisk the yolks, sugar, and juice together until smooth. Continue to cook, whisking constantly, until the mixture starts to thicken—but do not boil—about 10 minutes.
2. Remove the pan from the heat and let cool for 10 minutes. Whisk in the cold butter a little at a time until melted and smooth. Place the lemon curd in a glass container, cover tightly with plastic wrap, and chill thoroughly.

Chocolate Truffle Cake

LOMPOC CAFÉ, BAR HARBOR

serves 8

This dessert has been a mainstay at the Lompoc since the very beginning. Hard to believe this fudgelike flourless cake is so simple to make. Serve it on a plate drizzled with Raspberry or Caramel Rum Sauce and a spoonful of whipped cream.

½ cup (1 stick) butter, plus 2 tablespoons butter at room temperature
20 ounces semisweet chocolate chips
5 eggs

1. Preheat the oven to 425°F. Use the 2 tablespoons of soft butter to generously coat the bottom and sides of a 9-inch springform pan.
2. Melt the remaining ½ cup butter with the chocolate in a double boiler over hot but not boiling water. Stir frequently until the mixture is completely melted and smooth, then remove from the heat immediately and set aside. Cool slightly.
3. In a mixing bowl, use an electric mixer to beat the eggs until light and foamy. Gradually fold the chocolate mixture into the beaten eggs a little at a time until smooth.
4. Pour the batter into the prepared pan and bake for just 15 minutes. When the cake comes out of the oven, the center should not be completely firm and will appear to be undercooked. That's okay—it will remain creamy when the cake is cool.
5. Cool the cake to room temperature before slicing.

Raspberry Sauce

LOMPOC CAFÉ, BAR HARBOR

makes 3 cups

3 cups raspberries, fresh or frozen
1 teaspoon fresh-squeezed lemon juice
2 tablespoons superfine or powdered sugar, or more to taste

1. Place the berries, lemon juice, and sugar in a blender or food processor and purée until smooth.
2. Taste the mixture for sweetness. Add additional sugar, by the teaspoon, to taste.
3. Pour the sauce through a fine mesh strainer to remove all the seeds. Cover and refrigerate until ready to serve.

- Pancakes, waffles, and French toast
- Puddings and custards
- Cheesecake and pound cake
- Myrtle's Buttermilk Pie (see Index)

Caramel Rum Sauce

MARKET ON MAIN, ROCKLAND

makes 2 cups

Basic caramel—delicious over cakes, cheesecakes, ice cream, and more. Instead of rum, use bourbon, brandy, any whiskey, or flavored liqueur.

1 cup brown sugar
¼ cup (½ stick) butter
⅔ cup heavy or whipping cream
½ teaspoon vanilla extract
1 tablespoon dark rum, or a little more to taste

1. Combine the brown sugar, butter, and cream in a saucepan. Stir over low heat until the sugar has dissolved and the caramel is smooth.
2. Remove the pan from the heat and stir in the vanilla and rum.

Lunchtime, Market on Main

Five Cheesecakes

Plain Cheesecake

MARKET ON MAIN, ROCKLAND

serves 10–12

Basic Cheesecake Crust:

>   1 cup graham cracker crumbs
>   1 cup crushed vanilla wafers
>   ¼ cup (½ stick) butter, melted

Place the ingredients in a food processor and pulse just a few times to combine. Press the mixture into the bottom and sides of an 8- or 9-inch springform pan.

For the filling:

>   1 ½ pounds soft cream cheese
>   1 cup sour cream
>   1 cup sugar
>   1 tablespoon flour
>   1 teaspoon vanilla extract
>   3 eggs

1. Prepare the Basic Cheesecake Crust. Preheat the oven to 250°F.
2. Beat all the ingredients with an electric mixer, or by hand, until smooth.
3. Pour the filling into the prepared crust and slow-bake for 1 ½ hours.
4. Turn the oven off, leave the door partially opened, and leave the cake inside for 1 hour.
5. Remove the cake from the oven and cool to room temperature. Chill before serving.

Ginger Cheesecake

MARKET ON MAIN, ROCKLAND

serves 10–12

Add 3 tablespoons of finely minced crystallized ginger, plus 1/2 teaspoon dried ground ginger, to Plain Cheesecake filling.

Chocolate Swirl Cheesecake

MARKET ON MAIN, ROCKLAND

serves 10–12

1. Prepare Basic Cheesecake Crust and the filling for Plain Cheesecake.
2. Melt 4 ounces of good-quality semisweet chocolate and let cool slightly.
3. In a small bowl, blend the chocolate with 1 cup of the filling.
4. Pour the remaining filling into the prepared crust, then drop in the chocolate filling in a few large spoonfuls. Insert a knife into the filling and swirl the chocolate into the plain filling in a decorative pattern. Bake as directed for Plain Cheesecake.

Belgian Chocolate Cheesecake

COURTESY THE AUTHOR

serves 10–12

For the crust:

1 packet from a box of chocolate graham crackers
1 ½ tablespoons instant espresso granules (Ferrara brand is good)
¼ cup (½ stick) butter, melted then cooled

1. Coarsely break up the crackers and place them in the bowl of a food processor.
2. Add the instant espresso granules and pulse to make fine crumbs.
3. Drizzle in the butter and pulse again to combine.
4. Press the mixture into the bottom and sides of an 8- or 9-inch spring form pan.

For the filling:

8 ounces semisweet Belgian chocolate or other good-quality solid chocolate
2 ½ tablespoons instant espresso granules dissolved in ¼ cup hot water
1 ½ pounds soft cream cheese
2 cups sugar
2 eggs
½ cup sour cream

1. Preheat the oven to 350°F.
2. Melt the chocolate, then whisk in the coffee. Set aside to cool.
3. In a mixing bowl, beat the remaining ingredients until smooth. Add the chocolate mixture and stir until completely blended.
4. Pour the filling into the crust and bake for 40 to 50 minutes, until the filling is set and a tester inserted in the center comes out clean.
5. Cool the cheesecake to room temperature, then chill before serving.

Key Lime Cheesecake

LOMPOC CAFÉ, BAR HARBOR

serves 10–12

"The more you beat a cheesecake batter, the lighter the texture will be once the cake is baked. I prefer a dense, New York–style cheesecake, so I beat the ingredients just until they are fully blended. It's hard to obtain fresh key limes outside the Caribbean or the Florida Keys, but bottled key lime juice products can be found at specialty stores. I like Nellie and Joe's Famous Key West brand. Whatever you buy, be sure it's real key lime juice, not the doctored juice of regular limes."

—CHEF LISE DESROCHERS

Note: You can order Nellie and Joe's Famous Key West Lime Juice on the Internet at www.keylimejuice.com.

For the crust:

1 ¾ cups cinnamon graham cracker crumbs
5 tablespoons melted butter

For the filling:

1 ½ pounds (24 ounces) cream cheese, at room temperature
½ cup sugar
4 eggs
1 ½ teaspoons vanilla extract
6 tablespoons key lime juice (fresh or bottled; see Note)
finely grated zest from 2 key limes (or zest from 1 regular lime if using bottled lime juice)

For the sour cream topping:

2 cups sour cream
⅓ cup sugar
1 teaspoon vanilla extract

1. Preheat the oven to 350°F. Lightly grease a 10-inch springform pan.
2. Toss the graham cracker crumbs with the melted butter. Press the mixture into the bottom and halfway up the sides of the springform pan.
3. In a food processor, pulse the cream cheese and ½ cup sugar until smooth. Add the eggs, one at a time, blending briefly after each addition. Add the vanilla, lime juice, and zest and blend until smooth. Pour the batter slowly into the prepared crust and bake for 45 minutes.
4. To make the topping, whisk together the sour cream, ⅓ cup sugar, and vanilla. After the cheesecake has baked for 45 minutes, remove it from the oven, spread on the topping, then return the cheesecake to the oven and bake for another 6 to 8 minutes. Remove the cheesecake from the oven and allow it to cool to room temperature, then cover with plastic wrap and chill for 8 hours, or overnight, before serving.

Ginger Pear Cake with Caramel Rum Sauce

serves 8–10

1 ¼ cups sugar
⅓ cup chopped crystallized ginger
1 cup plus 2 tablespoons soft butter
2 large eggs
1 ½ cups molasses
4 ¼ cups flour
2 teaspoons baking soda
1 ½ teaspoons baking powder
1 tablespoon ground dried ginger
2 cups buttermilk
3 cups cubed peeled pears (¾-inch cubes)

1. Preheat the oven to 350°F. Generously butter a 9 x 13-inch glass baking dish.
2. Place the sugar and crystallized ginger in a food processor and pulse until the ginger is ground into small bits.
3. In a standing electric mixer, or by hand, cream the sugar-ginger mixture with the butter until light. Beat in the eggs, then the molasses.
4. Sift the dry ingredients together, then add to the batter by thirds, alternating with the buttermilk until just blended. Do not overbeat the cake.
5. Fold the cubed pears into the batter, then spread in the buttered baking dish.
6. Bake until a tester inserted in the center of the cake comes out clean, about 1 hour.
7. Serve the cake while still warm, cut into squares (topped with ice cream, if you like) and drizzled with warm Caramel Rum Sauce (see Index).

Pear, Cranberry, and Hazelnut Crisp

LOMPOC CAFÉ, BAR HARBOR

serves 6–8

This warm pear crisp can be made with any dried fruit you like: raisins, currants, cherries, blueberries…. Top the warm crisp with whipped cream or vanilla ice cream—and maybe a drizzle of Caramel Whiskey Sauce (see Index).

5 ripe, firm pears, peeled, cored, and cut into ½-inch-thick slices
½ cup sweetened dried cranberries
⅓ cup plus 2 tablespoons flour
½ cup rolled oats
½ teaspoon cinnamon
¼ teaspoon ground nutmeg
⅓ cup chopped hazelnuts
⅔ cup brown sugar
⅓ cup (⅔ stick) butter, at room temperature

1. Preheat the oven to 375°F.
2. In a mixing bowl, toss the sliced pears and cranberries with 2 tablespoons of the flour. Spread the mixture in a 10-inch-wide deep-dish pie plate.
3. In another bowl, combine the remaining ⅓ cup of flour with the remaining ingredients until crumbly. Using your fingers, distribute the mixture evenly over the fruit. Bake for 35 to 40 minutes, or until the pears are tender.

Wine-Poached Pears

THOMASTON CAFÉ, THOMASTON

serves 4

The trick is finding sweet, ripe pears that are still very firm.

4 fresh pears
1 cup sugar
1 cup water
½ cup dry red wine
coarse zest or peeling from 1 lemon
1 cinnamon stick
vanilla ice cream

1. Neatly peel the pears and core them from the bottom, leaving the stems intact.
2. In a saucepan just large enough to hold all the pears upright, dissolve the sugar in the water over medium heat. Add the wine, lemon zest, and cinnamon stick.

3. Place the pears side by side in the liquid, which should reach up to the stems. Bring to a boil, reduce the heat, and gently simmer for 15 to 20 minutes, or until the pears are cooked but still firm. Lift the pears from the pan and set aside to cool, then cover and chill.
4. Continue simmering the liquid until it is reduced to ½ cup of syrup. Serve the pears in dessert bowls with a scoop of vanilla ice cream drizzled with the wine syrup.

Wild Blueberry Cake with Lemon Glaze

LOMPOC CAFÉ, BAR HARBOR

serves 8–10

4 eggs, separated
2 cups sugar
1 cup vegetable shortening
2 teaspoons vanilla extract
½ teaspoon salt
2 teaspoons baking powder
½ teaspoon cinnamon
3 cups flour, plus 1 tablespoon
¾ cup milk
3 cups fresh or frozen blueberries

For the Lemon Glaze:

1 ½ cups powdered sugar, sifted
5 teaspoons fresh-squeezed lemon juice
1 tablespoon milk

1. Preheat the oven to 350°F. Grease and flour a 9 x 13-inch baking dish.
2. Using an electric mixer, beat the egg whites until foamy, then gradually add ½ cup of the sugar. Beat the whites until stiff peaks form, then set aside.
3. In another mixing bowl, using the mixer set to medium speed, beat the shortening until fluffy. Add the remaining sugar by spoonfuls, then the egg yolks one at a time, until incorporated. Add the vanilla, salt, baking powder, and cinnamon and beat until creamy.
4. Add the 3 cups of flour by thirds alternately with the milk, scraping down the sides of the bowl as you mix. With a large spatula, fold in the beaten egg whites. The batter will be very thick.
5. Put the blueberries and the remaining 1 tablespoon of flour in a large plastic bag and shake to coat the berries, then gently fold them into the batter.
6. Spread the batter into the prepared baking dish and bake for 45 minutes, or until a toothpick inserted in the center of the cake comes out clean. Let the cake cool while you make the glaze.
7. In a small bowl, blend the powdered sugar with the lemon juice and milk until smooth. When the cake is completely cool, spread the glaze evenly over the top. Allow the glaze to set for at least 30 minutes before cutting the cake into squares.

Creative Coastal Cooking

Myrtle's Buttermilk Pie

CAFÉ THIS WAY, BAR HARBOR

serves 6–8

This must be the world's easiest pie. It's delicious all by itself, but a dab of whipped cream and some fresh blueberries dress it up nicely. This is also known as Sugar Cream Pie in the Midwest and Chess Pie in the South, where it's customary to add a tablespoon of fresh lemon juice to the filling—which you can do if you like. Café This Way came by the recipe from their friend Myrtle of Cairo, Illinois—a great southern-style cook and a regular visitor to Bar Harbor.

> 1 single, unbaked piecrust to line a 9-inch pie pan
> 1 cup buttermilk
> 3 cups sugar
> 5 eggs
> ½ cup (1 stick) unsalted butter, melted and cooled
> 1 teaspoon vanilla extract
> 1 tablespoon fresh-squeezed lemon juice (optional)

1. Preheat the oven to 350°F. Line a 9-inch pie pan with the crust and crimp the edges.
2. In a mixing bowl, whisk together the remaining ingredients until smooth and pour into the unbaked pie shell. Carefully place the pie on a center oven rack and bake for about 1 hour, or until a toothpick inserted in the center of the pie comes out clean and the filling is firm. Cool the pie on a rack, then chill before serving.

Note: If you have the time, use scratch-made pie dough (see Index) for this single-crust pie. On the other hand, a ready-made crust from the supermarket will make a very good pie, ready for the oven in minutes.

Frances' Lime Coconut Pie

MARKET ON MAIN, ROCKLAND

serves 6

⅓ cup dried sweetened coconut
1 unbaked pastry shell in a 9-inch pie plate, well chilled
1 cup heavy cream, whipped to stiff peaks with 1 tablespoon sugar and
    1 teaspoon vanilla extract

For the filling:

1 cup dried sweetened coconut
4 large eggs, beaten
½ cup melted butter, cooled
1 cup sugar
½ teaspoon vanilla extract
¼ cup fresh-squeezed lime juice
finely grated zest of 1 lime

1. Preheat the oven at 400°F. Toast the ⅓ cup of coconut in the oven until just golden. Set aside until ready to serve the pie.
2. Whisk all the filling ingredients together until smooth. Pour into the chilled pie shell and bake for 10 minutes at 400°F, then reduce the oven temperature to 350°F and bake for an additional 20 minutes. The pie is done when the filling is set and a tester inserted in the center comes out clean.
3. Cool the pie to room temperature, then cover and refrigerate until well chilled, about 2 hours. Slice and serve topped with whipped cream and dusted with the toasted coconut.

Creative Coastal Cooking

Frances' Basic Pie Dough Pastry

MARKET ON MAIN, ROCKLAND

enough for a 2-crust pie

1 ⅓ cups flour
a scant pinch of salt
¼ cup vegetable shortening, chilled and cut into chunks
¼ cup butter, chilled and cut into chunks
6–8 tablespoons ice-cold water

Food processor method:

1. Place the flour, salt, and shortening chunks in the bowl of a food processor.
2. Pulse a few times, then scrape down the sides of the bowl.
3. Add the butter chunks and pulse again, just until the mixture resembles a very coarse, lumpy meal.
4. Add the water a tablespoon at a time, pulsing until the dough begins to hold together in a single ball.
5. Place the dough on a flour-dusted work surface and knead just a few turns, until it holds together enough to be rolled out flat.

By hand:

1. Place the flour and pinch of salt in a mixing bowl.
2. Use a pastry blender or large-tined fork to cut the shortening and butter into the flour.
3. Add the water a tablespoon at a time and continue to blend with the fork, or lightly with your fingers, until the dough begins to hold together in a ball.
4. Place the dough on a flour-dusted work surface and knead just a few turns, until it holds together enough to be rolled out flat.

Pie Crust How-To

The two key secrets to making good, flaky pie dough are:

- Use as little water as possible to make a viable dough.
- "Work" the dough as quickly and lightly as possible to form a pastry shell.

Pumpkin Bread Pudding with Hot Brown Sugar Sauce

LOMPOC CAFÉ, BAR HARBOR

serves 8–10

This pudding is definitely best served warm, though not necessarily the moment it emerges from the oven—it should rest for at least 15 or 20 minutes before you serve it. You can always reheat it with a bit of sauce in the microwave or the oven. The recipe can easily be halved.

For the Pumpkin Bread Pudding:

2 cups half-and-half
1 can (15 ounces) prepared pumpkin
1 cup packed brown sugar
4 large eggs
1 ½ teaspoons cinnamon
1 teaspoon ground ginger
¼ teaspoon ground nutmeg
¼ teaspoon ground allspice or cloves
1 ½ teaspoons vanilla extract
10 cups ½-inch cubes of good-quality white bread (a bit stale)

Preheat the oven to 350°F. In a large mixing bowl, whisk together the half-and-half, pumpkin, brown sugar, eggs, spices, and vanilla. Fold in the bread cubes and pour the mixture into a 9 x 13-inch glass baking dish. Let stand for 1 hour as the bread absorbs the liquids. Bake until a tester inserted in the center of the pudding comes out clean, about 40 minutes.

For the Hot Brown Sugar Sauce:

1 ¼ cups packed brown sugar
½ cup (1 stick) unsalted butter
½ teaspoon ground nutmeg
½ cup whipping cream, plus 1 additional cup for whipped cream topping

Whisk the brown sugar, butter, and nutmeg in a heavy saucepan over medium heat until the butter melts. Whisk in the ½ cup of cream and stir until the sugar dissolves and the sauce is smooth, about 3 minutes. Cut the warm pudding into squares and drizzle with sauce, accompanied by ice cream or whipped cream, if you like.

Maine Crazy Pudding

THOMASTON CAFÉ, THOMASTON

serves 8–10

Here's a gooey concoction best served with a big spoonful of whipped cream and a handful of fresh berries. Years ago Cathy Bellweather, head baker at Thomaston Café, got this recipe from a friend, and upon a first reading she said, "You're crazy! This will never work." But it does, and regulars at the Thomaston Café are crazy about it. The syrup saturates the batter as it bakes, making a saucy caramel pool under the pudding.

For the pudding:

1 cup sugar
¼ cup (½ stick) unsalted butter, soft
1 teaspoon salt
1 cup whole milk
2 cups all-purpose flour
2 teaspoons baking powder
2 teaspoons baking soda
1 teaspoon ground nutmeg
1 cup raisins (or other dried fruit; see Note)

For the syrup:

4 cups water
2 cups brown sugar
¼ cup (½ stick) unsalted butter
¼ cup fresh-squeezed lemon juice

1. Preheat the oven to 350°F. To make the pudding, cream together the sugar and soft butter. Add the remaining pudding ingredients and beat well with a spatula. Spread the batter into a 9 x 13-inch glass baking dish.
2. In a heavy saucepan, bring the 4 cups of water to a full boil. Add the remaining syrup ingredients and stir until the sugar is dissolved, about 3 minutes. Remove from the heat and pour the hot syrup evenly over the pudding batter. Bake for about 1 hour, until dark golden brown. The center should be "set" though not quite firm when the pudding is done. Let the hot pudding rest for at least 15 minutes before serving. Spoon into dessert bowls and top generously with whipped cream and berries.

Note: The pudding can be served warm or chilled. Any dried fruit will work: Think cranberries, cherries, blueberries, currants, chopped apricots, or dates.

"Gingerbread" Crazy Pudding

Get creative with Maine Crazy Pudding's spices. For a "gingerbread" version, add to the batter mixture:

- 1 ½ teaspoons ground ginger
- 1 ½ teaspoons cinnamon
- ½ teaspoon allspice
- ½ teaspoon ground nutmeg

Indian Pudding

THOMASTON CAFÉ, THOMASTON

serves 12

8 cups whole milk
1 ⅓ cups dark molasses
1 ⅓ cups yellow cornmeal
⅔ cup sugar
2 teaspoons salt
1 teaspoon cinnamon
1 teaspoon ground nutmeg
½ cup (1 stick) unsalted butter
cold whipped cream, for topping

1. Butter a 9 x 13-inch glass baking dish and preheat the oven to 300°F.
2. In a saucepan, heat 6 cups of the milk with the molasses. (Set aside the remaining 2 cups of milk.)
3. Add the cornmeal, sugar, salt, cinnamon, nutmeg, and butter. Simmer gently, stirring occasionally, for 10 minutes. Pour the mixture into the baking dish, then pour the reserved 2 cups of milk over it. Do not stir or mix.
4. Bake for 2 ½ to 3 hours. Remove the pudding from the oven while it is still wiggly on top. Serve warm with plenty of whipped cream.

Belgian Chocolate Drop Cookies

ROGUE RIVER CAFÉ, DAMARISCOTTA

makes 4 dozen

The bakers at Rogue River Café use organic flour and the fine couverture (bar) chocolate developed by the famous Callebaut family from Belgium, now widely available in the United States.

10 ounces semisweet Belgian chocolate
6 ounces unsweetened Belgian chocolate
¾ cup (1 ½ sticks) soft unsalted butter
4 large eggs
1 ½ cups brown sugar
½ cup granulated sugar
1 tablespoon vanilla extract
2 cups flour
½ cup cocoa powder
2 teaspoons baking powder
½ teaspoon salt
1 ½ cups semisweet or white chocolate chips (optional)

1. Preheat the oven to 350°F. Have ready two cookie sheets, lined with buttered waxed or parchment paper (or other nonstick liner).
2. Slowly melt the semisweet and unsweetened chocolates together in a heavy saucepan over low heat. Remove the pan from the heat and stir in the butter until smooth.
3. When the mixture has cooled for 15 minutes, whisk in the eggs one at a time, then mix in the sugars and vanilla.
4. Sift the dry ingredients together in a large mixing bowl. Blend in the chocolate mixture and the chocolate chips, if using. Drop by heaping tablespoons onto the cookie sheets and bake for about 15 minutes, or until the edges have just begun to brown but the centers are still soft.

Rogue River's Oatmeal Raisin Cookies

ROGUE RIVER CAFÉ, DAMARISCOTTA

makes 2 dozen

¾ cup (1 ½ sticks) soft unsalted butter
1 cup brown sugar
½ cup granulated sugar
2 large eggs
1 teaspoon vanilla extract
2 tablespoons finely grated orange zest
1 ½ cups flour
1 teaspoon baking soda
1 teaspoon baking powder
½ teaspoon salt
1 teaspoon cinnamon
½ teaspoon allspice
½ teaspoon ground nutmeg
2 ½ cups rolled oats
1 ½ cups raisins
1 cup chopped walnuts (optional)

1. Preheat the oven to 350°F.
2. In a mixing bowl, cream the butter and sugars together. Beat in the eggs until light. Stir in the vanilla and orange zest.
3. In another bowl toss together all the remaining ingredients until well blended. Add all the dry ingredients to the butter-egg mixture and combine with just a few turns of a spatula.
4. Using your hands, roll the cookie dough into balls just a bit larger than a golf ball. Arrange them on a greased or lined cookie sheet and press the balls lightly to flatten them a little. Bake until golden around the edges, about 10 minutes.

Creative Coastal Cooking

Sesame Cookies

BURNING TREE, BAR HARBOR

makes 2 dozen

Use up your favorite preserves to make these cookies for the holidays, or any time of year.

 1 cup (2 sticks) soft butter
 ¼ cup sugar
 1 teaspoon almond extract
 2 cups flour
 ½ teaspoon salt
 ½ cup sesame seeds
 ¼ cup jam or preserves

1. Preheat the oven to 400°F.
2. Cream the butter and sugar together until light and fluffy. Beat in the almond extract. Add the flour and salt and mix well.
3. Shape rounded tablespoons of the dough into smooth balls and roll in the sesame seeds to coat. Place on an ungreased cookie sheet.
4. With your thumb, indent the center of each cookie and fill with about ½ teaspoon of the jam or preserves. Bake for 10 to 12 minutes, or until the cookies are very lightly browned around the edges.

Chewy Molasses-Ginger Cookies

MORNING GLORY BAKERY, BAR HARBOR

makes 2 dozen

 ¾ cup (1 ½ sticks) soft butter
 1 cup granulated sugar
 ¼ cup brown sugar
 1 egg
 ½ cup molasses
 2 cups flour
 1 teaspoon baking powder
 1 tablespoon dried ginger
 2 ½ teaspoons cinnamon
 ¾ teaspoon ground nutmeg
 ¾ teaspoon ground cloves
 ¾ teaspoon salt
 ¼ teaspoon ground black pepper
 2 tablespoons minced fresh gingerroot
 1 ½ tablespoons unsweetened cocoa powder
 1 tablespoon brewed espresso

1. Preheat the oven to 375°F. Line a cookie sheet with waxed or parchment paper, or use a nonstick sheet.
2. Cream together the butter and sugars using an electric mixer, or by hand. Beat in the egg and molasses until light and fluffy.
3. In a large mixing bowl, sift together all the dry ingredients, including the spices. Fold in the wet ingredients, including the espresso, until blended.
4. Drop the cookie batter onto the baking sheet using a medium-sized ice cream scoop. Bake for about 12 minutes, or until the edges of the cookies are very lightly browned. Cool for 5 minutes on the baking sheet, then place the cookies on a cooling rack.

Extreme Brownies

MORNING GLORY BAKERY, BAR HARBOR

makes 15 big brownies

8 ounces good-quality unsweetened chocolate, broken into pieces
1 cup (2 sticks) butter
2 ½ cups sugar
1 teaspoon vanilla extract
6 eggs
1 cup flour

1. Preheat the oven to 375°F. Butter and flour one large baking pan, such as a lasagne pan, about 10 x 16 inches, or use two 9 x 9-inch square baking pans.
2. Heat the chocolate and butter together in a saucepan over very low heat, stirring until melted and smooth. Remove the pan from the heat.
3. Whisk in the sugar and vanilla until smooth. Beat in the eggs, one at a time. Fold in the flour with a few turns of a spatula until completely blended.
4. Spread the batter into the prepared baking dish, or dishes. Bake for 14 or 15 minutes, until the batter is set but not entirely firm. The brownie will hold together when they cool but remain moist and crumbly.
5. Cool the brownies in the pan completely before icing with Chocolate Ganache Icing.

For the Chocolate Ganache Icing:

1 cup half-and-half
4 cups bittersweet chocolate chips
2 tablespoons butter

1. Put the half-and-half in a large saucepan and bring just to the boiling point, then remove the pan from the heat. Whisk in the chocolate chips and butter until melted and smooth.
2. Allow the mixture to cool until it is just lukewarm and spreadable. Ice the brownies, then chill them before cutting them into squares.

Herbert's Classic Caramel Custards

THOMASTON CAFÉ, THOMASTON

makes 8 custards

Call it crème caramel or flan, this is the traditional golden brown custard dessert that you serve upside down in a pool of delicious caramel syrup—a perfect base for a spoonful of ripe blueberries or raspberries. No special tricks involved—here's how Herbert Peters makes it at Thomaston Café.

These custards are baked in a water bath, so have ready 8 ovenproof custard cups, a shallow roasting pan, and a kettle of boiling water.

For the caramel:

1 cup sugar
½ cup water

1. Preheat the oven to 325°F. Arrange the custard cups in the roasting pan.
2. In a heavy saucepan, heat the sugar and water until the sugar dissolves and the syrup begins to turn light golden brown. Be careful not to burn the syrup—remove the pan from the heat quickly when it's done.
3. Carefully spoon the hot caramel into the custard cups, then set them aside to cool while you make the custard.

For the custard:

8 large eggs
1 cup sugar
a scant pinch of salt
1 teaspoon vanilla extract
4 cups whole milk
ground nutmeg

1. Whisk together all the ingredients—except the nutmeg—until smooth.
2. Pour the custard evenly among the prepared cups and dust with nutmeg.
3. Place the roasting pan on the oven rack, then pour boiling water into the pan so that it reaches about halfway up the sides of the custard cups.
4. Bake for about 1 hour, or until the custard has set. Remove the custards from the pan and cool, then refrigerate until well chilled.
5. To serve, gently run a knife around the edge of each custard, then invert it onto a dessert plate. Serve plain, or garnish with fresh berries in season.

Ginger Cream Custards

MARKET ON MAIN, ROCKLAND

makes 6 servings

> 1 ½ cups whole milk
> 2 ⅔ cups heavy or whipping cream
> 2 tablespoons grated peeled fresh gingerroot
> 6 egg yolks
> 2 whole eggs
> ¾ cup sugar
> 1 teaspoon vanilla extract
> a scant pinch of salt

1. Preheat the oven to 325°F.
2. Combine the milk, cream, and ginger in a saucepan. Bring to a simmer and cook, uncovered, for 15 minutes. Remove the pan from the heat and allow the mixture to steep for at least 15 minutes.
3. Whisk together the egg yolks, eggs, sugar, vanilla, and salt until smooth. Slowly whisk in the cream mixture, then strain through a fine-mesh strainer.
4. Have ready a kettle of boiling water. Place 6 custard cups or ramekins in a large, deep baking pan. Distribute the custard equally among them. Place the baking pan on the oven rack, then pour in boiling water to reach halfway up the sides of the ramekins.
5. Bake until the custard is set, about 45 minutes to 1 hour. Cool the custards to room temperature, then chill before serving.

Creative Coastal Cooking

Chapter 8

The Chefs' Pantry

SALSAS AND CHUTNEYS, SPECIAL SAUCES,
STOCKS, AND SEASONINGS

The garden at Burning Tree

MOM's Year-Round Tomato Salsa

makes 4 ½ cups

2 cups drained canned tomatoes, seeded
½ cup minced red bell pepper
½ cup minced green pepper
2 fresh jalapeños, seeded and minced
2 tablespoons fresh-squeezed lime juice
1 teaspoon minced fresh garlic
1 teaspoon ground cumin
3 tablespoons olive oil
1 tablespoon minced fresh cilantro
salt and freshly ground black pepper to taste

Place the tomatoes in a food processor and pulse to chop, leaving plenty of chunky texture. Stir together with the remaining ingredients. Cover and allow the salsa to marinate for at least 1 hour, or overnight, before serving.

Salsa Fresca

COURTESY THE AUTHOR

makes about 2 cups

The most delicious and authentic of Mexican salsas, made with ripe summer tomatoes, fresh from the vine. Take care when handling the fresh jalapeños.

4 large tomatoes, quartered and seeded
½ cup grated sweet onion (such as Vidalia) with juices, plus ¼ cup finely
    chopped sweet onion
3 fresh jalapeño peppers
1 tablespoon fresh-squeezed lime juice, or substitute white vinegar
2 tablespoons minced fresh cilantro
salt and freshly ground black pepper to taste

1. Using the large holes on a handheld grater, scrape the flesh of the tomatoes away from the skins into a large bowl, catching all the tomato juices. Discard the skins. Stir in the grated onion, then place the mixture in a fine-mesh strainer and allow it to drain briefly to a thin salsa consistency.
2. Quarter the jalapeños lengthwise and remove the seeds. Using the fine holes of a handheld grater, grate the flesh away, working down to the skins. Discard the skins. (Wash your hands thoroughly when done!)
3. Blend the drained tomato mixture with the grated jalapeños and all the remaining ingredients. Season with salt and pepper to taste. Serve slightly chilled with salty tortilla chips.

Mango-Chile Salsa

CHERIE'S, KENNEBUNK

makes 2 ½ cups

This salsa is delicious served over grilled or pan-seared fish or chicken.

2 ripe mangoes
½ cup finely chopped red onion
1 serrano chile, seeded and minced
2 tablespoons peanut oil
1 tablespoon water
¼ cup minced fresh mint leaves
2 tablespoons fresh-squeezed lime juice
½ teaspoon salt
½ teaspoon freshly ground black pepper

1. Peel and dice the mangoes. Set aside in a mixing bowl.
2. In a small saucepan, combine the onion, chile, oil, and water. Cover and simmer over low heat for 5 minutes (do not brown the onion). Let stand until completely cool.
3. Add the onion mixture, along with the mint, lime juice, salt, and pepper, to the mangoes. Toss to combine, cover, and refrigerate for at least 1 hour before serving.

Eggplant Salsa

LOMPOC CAFÉ, BAR HARBOR

makes 3 cups

This salsa is something like Italian caponata, an eggplant relish, and can be used as a dip for tortilla chips, a spread, a pizza topping—use your imagination. Make it a day or two in advance to let the eggplant mellow as it absorbs the other flavors. Serve at room temperature with tortilla or pita chips, or warm crusty bread.

¼ cup olive oil
1 cup chopped onion
¼ cup chopped green pepper
2 ½ cups cubed peeled eggplant
1 teaspoon minced fresh garlic
¾ cup canned crushed tomatoes
¾ cup chopped mushrooms
¼ cup pimiento-stuffed green olives, drained
2 tablespoons balsamic vinegar
1 teaspoon dried oregano
½ teaspoon freshly ground black pepper

1. Heat the oil in a skillet and sauté the onion and green pepper for 5 minutes. Add the eggplant and continue to sauté, until tender, about 10 minutes more.
2. Add the remaining ingredients, lower the heat, and simmer, uncovered, for 15 to 20 minutes, stirring often.
3. Remove the pan from the heat and cool to room temperature. In a food processor, pulse the salsa a few times to break it up a bit, taking care to retain a chunky texture.
4. To serve, put the salsa in a decorative bowl and drizzle with a little additional olive oil.

Mojo Sauce

LOCAL 188, PORTLAND

makes 2 cups

Mojo is the "salsa" of the Canary Islands. At Local 188, it's served with pan-seared fish, on grilled chicken or shrimp, and as dip for french-fried or roasted potatoes.

½ cup chopped red or Spanish onion
1 teaspoon chopped fresh garlic
2–4 teaspoons sherry vinegar
1 roasted red bell pepper, peeled and seeded
1 fresh red bell pepper, seeded and diced
1 tablespoon minced fresh cilantro
1 teaspoon hot, smoky paprika
2 chopped scallions
salt and cayenne pepper to taste

1. Place the onion, garlic, 2 teaspoons of vinegar, and half the roasted red pepper in a food processor and pulse until almost puréed.
2. Add the remaining ingredients and pulse to a salsalike consistency. Season with additional vinegar, salt, and cayenne to taste.

Lemon Aioli for Grilled or Fried Seafood

MARKET ON MAIN, ROCKLAND

makes 3 cups

1 ½ cups mayonnaise
1 cup sour cream
¼ teaspoon cayenne
1 teaspoon mashed fresh garlic
1 tablespoon minced flat-leaf parsley
2 tablespoons olive oil
¼ cup fresh lemon juice, or more to taste
salt to taste

Whisk all the ingredients together until smooth. Add more lemon juice and/or salt to taste. Cover and chill for at least 1 hour before serving.

Lemon-Caper Tartar Sauce

MARKET ON MAIN, ROCKLAND

makes 2 cups

1 cup mayonnaise
½ cup sour cream
2 tablespoons fresh-squeezed lemon juice
¼ cup extra-virgin olive oil
1 teaspoon prepared Dijon mustard
1 tablespoon drained capers
½ cup coarsely chopped flat-leaf parsley
1 teaspoon minced fresh garlic

Place all the ingredients in a food processor and pulse just a few times to combine, leaving a chunky texture.

MOM's Red Pepper Mayonnaise for Seafood

makes 3 cups

2 cups mayonnaise
½ cup sour cream
½ cup finely diced roasted red bell peppers
1 teaspoon finely minced fresh garlic
2 tablespoons fresh lemon juice
2 tablespoons olive oil
a large pinch of cayenne, or more to taste

Whisk all the ingredients until blended. Cover and refrigerate.

Spanish Romesco Sauce

LOCAL 188, PORTLAND

makes about 2 ½ cups

Romesco is the favorite sauce of Spain, and there are as many ways to make it as there are Spaniards. The basic ingredients are almonds, roasted red peppers, garlic, and bread cubes toasted in lots of olive oil, all puréed to a smooth consistency. It is traditionally eaten with grilled fish, but works as a dip or condiment for all kinds of grilled or fried meat, seafood, and vegetable dishes.

½ cup plus 2 tablespoons Spanish olive oil
10 whole cloves fresh garlic, peeled
1 cup cubed good-quality bread
½ cup peeled, blanched almonds
4 whole peeled plum tomatoes (fresh or canned), seeded
1 roasted red bell pepper, peeled and seeded (see Index)
2–3 tablespoons sherry vinegar
salt and freshly ground black pepper to taste

1. Heat the ½ cup of olive oil in a skillet. Add the garlic cloves and cook over low heat until soft and brown. Lift the cloves from the hot oil and set aside. Reserve the oil from the skillet in a measuring cup and set aside to cool to room temperature.
2. Toss the bread cubes in the remaining 2 tablespoons of oil, then sauté until golden brown. Set aside on a plate to cool.
3. Put the almonds in the hot skillet and sauté over low heat until toasted. Set aside to cool.

4. When the garlic, bread cubes, and almonds are completely cooled, put them in a food processor and purée until smooth. Add the tomatoes, roasted red pepper, and vinegar and purée. With the motor running, drizzle in the reserved oil to make a thick emulsion.
5. Season to taste with additional salt and/or vinegar and pepper.

Saffron Tomato Sauce

LOCAL 188, PORTLAND

makes 5 cups

This is a fundamental sauce recipe for the Spanish-inspired cooking at Local 188. It's used in soups as well as on meats, fish, pasta, eggs, and more.

1 tablespoon olive oil
1 cup finely diced Spanish onion
2 cans (28 ounces each) peeled whole plum tomatoes
28 ounces water
1 tablespoon minced fresh garlic
2 teaspoons saffron threads, crushed
salt and freshly ground black pepper to taste

1. Heat the olive oil in a large soup pot. Add the onion and cook over medium-low heat until translucent.
2. Add the canned tomatoes, along with their canned juices. Refill 1 can with water and add to the pot.
3. Add the garlic and saffron and stir. Bring the sauce to a boil, lower the heat, and simmer, uncovered, until the sauce is reduced by half.

David Noyes and Jay Villani, Local 188

Apple and Onion Chutney

MARKET ON MAIN, ROCKLAND

makes about 2 ½ cups

1 tablespoon olive oil
1 cup diced Spanish onion
4 Granny Smith apples, peeled, cored, and diced
¾ cup brown sugar
¾ cup cider or champagne vinegar
1 tablespoon black mustard seeds
1 cinnamon stick
⅓ teaspoon red pepper flakes

1. Heat the olive oil in a saucepan and sauté the onion for 5 minutes.
2. Add the remaining ingredients, stir, and bring the mixture to a boil. Reduce the heat to low and simmer for 30 to 40 minutes. Serve the chutney at room temperature.

Blueberry Chutney

CAFÉ THIS WAY, BAR HARBOR

makes 3 cups

Serve alongside grilled or roasted poultry or pork.

2 teaspoons vegetable oil
½ cup finely diced white onion
1 tablespoon finely grated fresh gingerroot
¾ cup brown sugar
½ cup red wine vinegar
2 cups fresh blueberries

1. Heat the oil in small saucepan. Add the onion and ginger and cook for 5 minutes over low heat.
2. Add the brown sugar, vinegar, and blueberries. Bring to a simmer and cook, uncovered, until reduced and thickened, about 15 minutes.
3. Let cool to room temperature, then cover and refrigerate until ready to use.

Cranberry Citrus Relish

PRIMO, ROCKLAND

makes about 3 cups

A relish to serve alongside roasted poultry or pork.

1 pound fresh cranberries, roughly chopped
1 cup sugar
1 lemon, 1 orange, and 1 lime, each seeded and chopped, rinds and all

Put all the ingredients in a saucepot, bring to a boil, and reduce to a simmer. Cook the relish, uncovered, until it's reduced and thickened. Serve cold or at room temperature.

Lompoc Chutney

LOMPOC CAFÉ, BAR HARBOR

makes about 3 cups

"We have an apple tree in our garden at the Lompoc, and it sets fruit every other year. When we can, we use the apples from it, which are firm and tart. Granny Smiths are a good substitute. We serve this chutney with Smoked Cheddar Boursin (see Index) on roasted chicken, but it would be great with roasted pork or duck, or as a snack with a good, sharp Cheddar and whole-grain crackers."

—CHEF LISE DESROCHERS

3 Granny Smith apples, cored, peeled, and diced
½ cup finely chopped red bell pepper
½ cup finely chopped red onion
½ cup cider vinegar
½ cup packed brown sugar
1 ½ teaspoons minced garlic
1 ½ teaspoons grated fresh gingerroot
¼ cup dried currants
¼ cup dried cranberries
a large pinch each of ground cayenne, cloves, and allspice
¼ teaspoon salt
¼ teaspoon ground black pepper

Combine all the ingredients in a saucepan, and bring to a boil over medium heat. Simmer for 25 minutes, uncovered, stirring occasionally. Let cool a little, then chill tightly covered.

Rhubarb Chutney

LOMPOC CAFÉ, BAR HARBOR

makes about 3 cups

"Rhubarb, along with strawberries and asparagus, is a sure sign to us here in Maine that summer truly will arrive. This sweet-tart chutney is excellent on grilled chicken or pork, or served with goat cheese, French bread, and a California Chardonnay as an early-summer evening appetizer."

—CHEF LISE DESROCHERS

6 tablespoons sugar
2 ½ tablespoons cider vinegar
2 teaspoons grated fresh gingerroot
1 ½ teaspoons minced fresh garlic
½ teaspoon ground cumin
1/4 teaspoon cinnamon
¼ teaspoon ground cloves
a pinch of crushed red pepper flakes, or more to taste
2 cups chopped rhubarb
¼ cup chopped red onion
⅓ cup dried cherries

In a saucepan, heat the sugar and vinegar, stirring, until the sugar is dissolved. Add all the remaining ingredients, stir to combine, and simmer until the rhubarb is tender but still firm. Let the chutney cool to room temperature, then store in the refrigerator in a jar or other airtight container.

Sun-Dried Tomato and Roasted Almond Pesto

ROGUE RIVER CAFÉ, DAMARISCOTTA

makes about 1 ½ cups

This nutty "pesto" is a great spread for hot sandwiches, especially with grilled portobello mushrooms. It's also an excellent vegetable dip.

5 ounces whole almonds, organic if available
4 ounces sun-dried tomatoes (dry-pack type, not reconstituted)
1 small clove fresh garlic
¼ teaspoon salt
¼ teaspoon fennel seeds
½ cup plus 1 tablespoon olive oil

1. Preheat the oven to 300°F. Spread the almonds on a baking sheet and toast for about 15 minutes, until golden brown. Cool the nuts to room temperature.
2. Pulse the almonds and sun-dried tomatoes in a food processor until coarsely chopped.
3. Add the garlic, salt, and fennel seeds and pulse to blend. With the motor running, drizzle in the olive oil until the pesto is somewhat smooth, but with bits of almond still visible.

Basil-Arugula Pesto

COURTESY THE AUTHOR

makes 1 ½–2 cups

1 cup packed fresh basil leaves, rinsed and dried
1 cup packed arugula, stemmed, rinsed, and dried
1 tablespoon chopped fresh garlic
½ cup pine nuts, lightly toasted
¼ cup finely grated Reggiano Parmesan cheese
½ cup extra-virgin olive oil
salt and freshly ground black pepper to taste

Place all the ingredients in a food processor and pulse until smooth. Season with just a little salt and plenty of black pepper.

Pesto Uses

This versatile basic pesto has countless uses and keeps well in the freezer.

- Toss with hot or chilled pasta for a main course.
- Add to cream sauces for pasta.
- Add to soups, stews, and vinaigrettes as a seasoning.
- Blend with soft goat cheese or cream cheese to make a spread.
- Blend with mayonnaise as a seafood sauce or sandwich spread.

Caramelized Onions

Onions, when patiently sautéed over very low heat for a long time, release their natural sugars—which turn into a sweet brown glaze. Total cooking time is 1 hour minimum; 2 hours if you have the time and patience. The longer the onions cook, the sweeter they will be.

2 large Spanish onions
1 tablespoon bacon drippings or olive oil
¼ teaspoon kosher or sea salt (omit if using bacon drippings)
1 tablespoon balsamic vinegar

1. Peel the onions and cut into ¼-inch-thick slices.
2. Heat the bacon drippings or olive oil in a large skillet.
3. Add the onions and toss with the salt and oil. As soon as the onions begin to turn golden, turn the heat down as low as possible.
4. Continue to cook the onions, stirring often, for 1 hour. Add the balsamic vinegar and cook for an additional 30 minutes or more.

Uses for Caramelized Onions

- As a topping for "white" pizza, along with crumbled Gorgonzola and pine nuts.
- Served over grilled or roasted meats.
- On Roasted Cheese Plates (see Index).
- Added to fettuccine Alfredo or other creamy pasta dishes.
- Chilled, on green salads.
- In omelets.
- On sandwiches.
- Tossed with cooked green beans or asparagus.

Roasted Garlic

HERE ARE A COUPLE OF RECOMMENDED METHODS FROM CHEF KERRY ALTIERO AT CAFÉ MIRANDA.

To make roasted garlic in a hurry, place a whole head of garlic in a glass dish with 2 tablespoons of water, cover tightly with plastic wrap, and microwave for 3 minutes. For basic oven-roasted garlic, trim a slice about 1/8 inch thick from the top of the garlic bulb to expose the inner cloves. Place on a sheet of foil, drizzle with 1 tablespoon olive oil, and wrap tightly. Place in a 375°F oven for 30 minutes.

With either method, be sure to let the garlic cool before you try to handle it. The cloves should be very soft and will squeeze right out of their skins.

Roasted Red Peppers

HERE'S A BASIC METHOD FOR ROASTING AND PEELING ANY PEPPER.

1. Preheat the oven broiler—use the highest setting.
2. Place the peppers on an oven rack within 6 or 8 inches of the heat.
3. Allow the outer skins of the peppers to become puffy and charred, turning them several times with kitchen tongs to char them on all sides.
4. When the peppers are done, place them in a large plastic bag and seal the bag tightly.
5. As the peppers cool, the steam will cook them.
6. When the peppers are completely cool, cut or split them into sections, removing all the seeds and pulling away the skins.
7. Drain the peppers, drizzle with a little olive oil, cover, and refrigerate.

All-Purpose Smoky Spice Blend

COURTESY THE AUTHOR

makes ¾ cup

Chili powder from ground chipotle peppers lends a smoky aroma to this spice blend.

1 tablespoon brown sugar, light or dark
1 ½ tablespoons chipotle chili powder
2 tablespoons sweet or mild paprika
2 tablespoons granulated garlic
2 tablespoons granulated onion
3 tablespoons salt
2 tablespoons ground black pepper
2 teaspoons ground cumin
2 teaspoons cayenne
2 teaspoons crushed dried thyme leaves

Smoky Spice Blend Uses

- Give steaks, chicken, or fish a generous coating before grilling.
- Add to soups, stews, sauces, and salsas.
- Add to scrambled eggs or omelets.
- Add to tartar sauce or other mayonnaise-based condiments.

Basic Chicken Stock

COURTESY THE AUTHOR

makes 8 cups

3 pounds chicken backs, wings, or other scraps
1 cup coarsely diced onion
1 cup coarsely diced celery, including green leafy tops
2 carrots, peeled and diced
1 bay leaf
1 teaspoon dried thyme
1 teaspoon black peppercorns
12 cups water

1. Place all the ingredients in a large soup or stockpot. Bring to a boil.
2. Gently simmer over low heat, partially covered, for 2 ½ hours. Every 20 minutes or so, use a wide metal spoon to skim any foam away from the surface of the stock.
3. Strain the stock through a fine-mesh strainer. To degrease the stock, use a gravy separator, or put the stock in the refrigerator then skim away the fat that will rise to the surface once the stock is cold.

Basic Beef Stock

makes 8 cups

1 large onion, peeled and thickly sliced
3 stalks celery, thickly sliced
4 large garlic cloves, peeled and chopped
3 carrots, peeled and coarsely chopped
½ cup chopped red bell pepper
3 tablespoons vegetable oil
2 bay leaves
2 teaspoons dried thyme
1 teaspoon black peppercorns
2 teaspoons sugar
3 pounds meaty beef bones
12 cups water

1. Preheat the oven to 450°F. Spread the vegetables in a large roasting pan. Drizzle on the oil, then add the bay leaves, thyme, peppercorns, and sugar. Toss the mixture.
2. Lay the beef bones over the vegetables and bake for 1 hour, stirring occasionally.
3. Remove all the ingredients from the roasting pan and place them in a large stock- or soup pot. Add 1 cup of the water to the roasting pan and stir, scraping up all the brown bits, and add to the stockpot.
4. Add the remaining 11 cups of water to the pot and bring to a boil. Lower the heat and simmer, partially covered; every 20 minutes or so, use a wide metal spoon to skim away any foam from the surface of the stock. Continue simmering for 2 ½ to 3 hours, or until the stock develops a good rich flavor. Remove the pot from the heat and let cool to room temperature.
5. Strain the stock through a fine-mesh strainer. To degrease the stock, use a gravy separator, or put the stock in the refrigerator then skim away the fat that will rise to the surface once the stock is cold.

Basic Fish Stock

STREET & CO., PORTLAND

makes 5 cups

Fish "rack" is what's left after the fishmonger is done carving away the fillets: fish heads, bones, skin, and tails.

1 cup diced onion
½ cup diced celery
2 teaspoons olive oil
1 ½ pounds very fresh fish rack
1 teaspoon dried thyme
1 teaspoon fennel seeds, lightly crushed
2 bay leaves
1 cup dry white wine
5 cups water

1. In a stockpot, sauté the onion and celery in the olive oil until soft, about 10 minutes.
2. Add the fish rack and all the remaining ingredients. Bring to a boil, lower the heat, and simmer for 30 minutes, skimming the away any foam that rises to the surface with a wide, flat spoon.
3. Pour the stock through a fine-mesh strainer, pressing the solids with the back of a spoon to extract as much flavorful liquid as possible. Cover and refrigerate or freeze the stock until ready to use.

Recipe Index

Index of People and Places